EMIGRANTS FROM IRELAND, 1847-1852

State-Aided Emigration Schemes from Crown Estates in Ireland

BY EILISH ELLIS

CLEARFIELD

Originally published as, "State-Aided Emigration Schemes
from Crown Estates in Ireland c. 1850"
in *Analecta Hibernica*, No. 22
Dublin, 1960

Excerpted and reprinted by Genealogical Publishing Co., Inc.
Baltimore, Maryland
1977, 1978, 1983, 1993

Library of Congress Catalog Card Number 76-39654

Reprinted for Clearfield Company by
Genealogical Publishing Company
Baltimore, Maryland
2014

ISBN 978-0-8063-0748-0

STATE-AIDED EMIGRATION SCHEMES
FROM CROWN ESTATES IN IRELAND
c. 1850

Presented by

EILISH ELLIS, M.A.

INTRODUCTORY NOTE

By resolution of the Irish Manuscripts Commission of 19 June 1945, it was decided to publish in *Analecta Hibernica* a set of documents illustrative of state-aided emigration schemes from crown estates in Ireland, c. 1850.

Attention had been directed to these documents by Dr. R. C. Simington of the Commission. Already, in 1927, at the request of the late James F. Kenney of the Public Archives of Canada, an investigation was made into documents in the Quit Rent Office, Dublin, which contained information relating to persons assisted to emigrate to North America from crown estates in Ireland. This investigation revealed the existence of a collection of material relating to the estates of Ballykilcline, Co. Roscommon; Irvilloughter and Boughill, Co. Galway; Kilconcouse, Offaly; Kingwilliamstown, Co. Cork, and Castlemaine, Co. Kerry. (By the courtesy of the then Superintendant of the Quit Rent Office, the late G. H. Burnett, copies of portions of this material were sent to Dr. Kenney).[1]

The emigration schemes had been carried out under the direction of the Commissioners of Woods, Forests and Land Revenues of the Crown,[2] whose office was in London, and under whom the Quit Rent Office, Dublin, functioned from 1827.[3] Some material relating to the schemes had been sent to the Quit Rent Office from the Office of Woods after the transfer of the land revenues of the Crown to the Irish Free State from 31 March 1923.

The Quit Rent Office collection of books and papers was removed to the Public Record Office, Dublin, in 1943, on the transfer of the Quit Rent Office to the Land Commission, and a MS index to it has been compiled by Miss Margaret Griffith, Deputy-keeper, and other

---

[1] A typescript copy of the material sent to Canada is preserved in the Q.R.O. file 11821.

[2] Hereinafter referred to as Commissioners of Woods or Office of Woods.

[3] The Commissioners of Woods were then of quite recent origin having been appointed in 1810, (50 Geo. III. c. 65), for the purpose of the management of the revenues derived from Crown lands in England ; they succeeded the 'Court of General Surveyors' one of whom was a surveyor-general of the land revenues and the other of woods and forests. In 1832 it was considered expedient to unite the department of the Surveyor–General of Works and Public Buildings with that of the Commissioners of Woods. Under the title, Commissioners of Woods, Forests, Land Revenues, Works and Buildings, this union lasted until 1851 when they were again divided, (14 & 15 Vic. c. 42).

The Quit Rent Office derived its title from one of the hereditary revenues of the Crown, viz. quit rents which arose mainly from grants of land after the

5

members of the staff. The documents in the Public Record Office dealing specifically with emigration from the crown estates are found in the bundles of loose papers, indexed under the name of each particular estate, (e.g., Correspondence relating to King-williamstown), as well as in the letter books of the Quit Rent Office and the Office of Woods, London, and in the files of the Forfeiture Office.

This collection provides much material which would be of interest to the student of social and economic conditions in 19th century Ireland. There are references to trades and occupations, farming methods, the rundale system, the evils of the land system and proposed remedies. Several excellent maps and tracings of estates, as well as plans of houses to be erected as part of crown improvements, are readily available. There is information too on the erection of schools under the Commissioners of National Education, on the erection of churches and rectories, bridges and roads, railways and canals. Eye-witnesses' accounts of the progress of the famine are available in the petitions for relief and in the letters from local relief committees. There is also material relating to the working of the Poor Law.

The present report consists of :—

I. A note on the emigration scheme and a list of the emigrants from each estate. These as here presented are compiled from :—

(a) Preliminary lists of potential emigrants from each estate, compiled at the request of the clerk of the Quit Rent Office, Dublin, or the Commissioners of Woods in London, by a local crown official, giving details of name, age, with, in some cases, additional information as to occupancy of land and occupation.

(b) Shipping-agents' receipted accounts containing the names to whom sailing tickets were issued, the ticket numbers and the family groupings; the number of adults and children with

---

Restoration of Charles II. These rents, of a confirmatory nature from the Commonwealth period and earlier, were regulated by the Acts of Settlement and Explanation. In 1669 hereditary revenues (including customs and excise), were set to farm. When this procedure ended shortly before 1688, the system of collection (including the office of Clerk of the Quit Rents) established by the farmers was adopted by government and entrusted to the Commissioners of Revenue.

Some lands forfeited in 1641 and not disposed of by the Crown at the Restor-ation were subsequently leased subject to rents; likewise lands forfeited in 1688 which had remained undisposed of after the sales by the Trustees of Forfeited Estates in 1703, were leased by the Commissioners of Revenue. Prior to the transfer to the Commissioners of Woods in 1827, the collection of the Irish land revenues had been entrusted to the Commissioners of Excise in succession to the General Board of Revenue abolished in 1806.

the appropriate fare; the cost of provisions, tins and cooking utensils supplied, and the amount of 'landing money' and commission payable at the port of disembarkation.

(c) Receipted accounts of 'landing-money' paid by agents of the shipping companies in New York and Quebec.

(d) Returns and clearance papers from emigration officers at the port of embarkation.

(e) Expense accounts of the local official in charge of travel arrangements to the port of embarkation.

(f) Inter-departmental letters between the offices of the Commissioners of Woods, Emigration, the Quit Rent Office and the Treasury.

(g) Miscellaneous letters and memorials from tenants, local landlords and agents.

II. A collection of four letters from emigrants written shortly after their arrival in the United States. These are printed verbatim with spelling and punctuation as in the originals.

The manuscripts, letter-books and papers, which are used, are cited according to the MS index to the Quit Rent Office collection in the Public Record Office, Dublin.

When available, the names of emigrants from each estate are presented in alphabetical order under the following headings :—

(a) Name : In this column the heads of the family are placed first; then come the male members of the family with christian names in alphabetical order, followed by females. A relative of the same surname is placed last in the family group.

(b) Details of age.

(c) Additional information : This column is used to indicate family relationships and any other information available. (The letters in section II supply information as to where some of the emigrants settled in America.)

(d) Date of departure from port of embarkation.

(e) Date of arrival in North America.

(f) Name of ship.

EVENTS LEADING TO THE ADOPTION OF STATE-AIDED EMIGRATION SCHEMES

The estates from which state-aided emigration took place were part of crown property in Ireland the management of which was one of the functions of the Quit Rent Office. They had been let on various long term leases which expired or were terminated in the early 1830's when it was discovered that a considerable population dependent on uneconomic holdings had accumulated on the estates, e.g., Ballykilcline. A survey of this estate made in 1836 revealed that there were 463 subdivisions and a population of just over 500 on a farm of approximately 602 acres. The impossibility of instituting improvements under these conditions of over-population is apparent, and, with the possible exception of the model farm experiment at Kingwilliamstown, little was done under the Commissioners of Woods in the years before the famine to solve the problems arising from the dependence of an ever-increasing population on an over-worked and worn-out soil.

That emigration would provide an outlet was recognised at least as early as 1836, when a census of the population of Irvilloughter was made by order of the Commissioners of Woods, with this end in view. The tenants refused the offer to help them emigrate and twelve years were to elapse before they themselves petitioned the Commissioners to be sent to America.

The immediate cause of the inauguration of the state-aided emigration scheme was the necessity for providing some relief for a group of Ballykilcline tenants evicted after protracted court proceedings for non-payment of rent. They petitioned the Commissioners of Woods on 28 May 1847, asking either that they be allowed to re-occupy their holdings, or, that 'the means of emigration on a scale similar to that lately practised by the landlords in this vicinity' be provided for them. The Commissioners almost immediately authorised the clerk of the Quit Rents to make arrangements for the departure, not only of those willing to emigrate, but of those who had lately been evicted. The failure of the potato crop, 1845-7, was the reason for the extension of the scheme to the estates of Irvilloughter and Boughill. Between 1847 and 1852, while state-aided emigration was in progress, just over eleven hundred people left these five crown estates in Ireland to settle in Canada and the United States.

The implementation of the scheme for the estates of Ballykilcline, Boughill, Irvilloughter and Kilconcouse was entrusted to John Burke, clerk of the Quit Rents, who was assisted by the crown agent or collector of excise for the district in which the particular estate was situated. Michael Boyan, superintendent of Kingwilliamstown model farm, was responsible for the scheme for that estate and for Castlemaine, under the direct control of the Commissioners. It may be noted that more complete details are available for those estates for which Burke was responsible.

Two separate lists of names were compiled by the supervisor of the emigration scheme for each particular estate. The first, consisting of those who had signified their intention of emigrating or who had been compulsorily ejected, was necessary for assessing the amount of money required from the Treasury. It sometimes differed from the second list which gave the names of those who actually left, and which was compiled on or shortly before the day of departure for the port of embarkation. Both lists were sent either direct to the office of the Commissioners of Woods in London, or to the clerk of the Quit Rents in Dublin who forwarded copies to the Commissioners. The second list was checked later with the returns from the shipping agents and the emigration officials at New York and Quebec. It is thus possible to arrive at an almost exact figure of the number of emigrants and be assured of reasonable accuracy in the lists of names.

NOTE ON THE EMIGRATION SCHEME FROM BALLYKILCLINE

The crown estate of Ballykilcline was situated in the parish of Kilglass in the barony of Ballintubber, Co. Roscommon. It contained about 602 acres sub-divided into very minute holdings occupied by 'cottier labourers', and was almost completely over-tilled and worn out when the lease to the tenant, Lord Hartland, fell in in April, 1834. Before the expiration of the lease, terms for the sale of the property had been proposed to Lord Hartland who did not accept them, and the rents, which appeared to have been paid regularly to his agent, were placed in charge with the agents of the Commissioners of Woods, from 1 May 1834.[4] Though the annual amount payable by the under-tenants, of whom there were 74, amounted to £411 19s. 11d., less than £350 had been collected when the payment of all rents ceased from 1836. Notices to quit were served and possession demanded from the tenants, and by 1 May 1837, 56 holdings had been surrendered. The remainder however, refused, and in the spring of 1842, John Burke, clerk of the Quit Rent Office, proposed their eviction after a visit to the estate.[5]

There was considerable opposition to the attempts made by crown officials to enter the estate; the assistance of the police was necessary on several occasions;[6] houses were re-occupied and bailiffs attacked when serving eviction notices.[7] However, those charged with assaulting the bailiffs were acquitted by a jury, who, in the opinion of the crown agent, 'were a set of the *lamest* and most ignorant men could be impanelled, and a disgrace to any Court of Justice'.[8] The establishment of a police barracks on the estate was considered at one stage, so determined was the resistance.[9]

It was not until it became evident that there was organised opposition among the tenantry that the Commissioners of Woods

---

4 Q.R.O., O.W. Land Revenue Series Letter Books, memo of James Weale, surveyor for Commissioners of Woods, 2 April 1834. Mr. Weale was a zealous collector of papers relating to Ireland. His MS purchases at the sale of Lord de Clifford's library in 1834 included "The History of the Survey of Ireland commonly called the Down Survey by Doctor William Petty", which was later edited by Larcom for the Irish Archaeological Society (1851). Mr. Weale died in 1838.

5 *Ibid.* Burke to Commissioners of Woods, 28 February 1842. In a letter of 23 December 1841 to the Commissioners, Burke vehemently opposed the letting of the land to a middleman who might be compelled to resort to eviction of an 'immense population'.

6 *Ibid.*, R. Hamilton & Co., crown solicitors, to Burke, 27 April 1842.

7 *Ibid.*, Michael Ryan, Quit Rent driver, to John Tuck, collector of excise, Athlone, 13 March 1844; George Knox, crown agent, to Burke, 10 May 1844.

8 *Ibid.*, George Knox to Burke, 9 July 1844.

9 *Ibid.*, Commissioners of Woods to Burke, 29 May 1844.

grew impatient. It was reported that the tenants had employed a lawyer named Hugh O'Farrell, whom they were paying at the rate of five shillings per acre each, to prevent their being evicted. A party of 'Molly Maguires' also visited the estate.[10]

A decree in favour of the Crown was obtained in April, 1846,[11] and on May 12, petitions were received from the tenants through their agent, Hugh O'Farrell, and the O'Conor Don, asking for leases under the Crown. The Lord Lieutenant, Lord Bessborough, also pleaded for a year's grace, and on 19 June 1846, the Commisioners of Woods expressed their willingness to grant tenancies on condition that two years rent be paid beforehand by those against whom decrees were obtained. The year's grace expired and steps were taken to execute the writ of possession. An army of 60 police, 25 cavalry, 30 infantry and a stipendiary magistrate were deemed necessary as an escort for the sheriff, and on 27 May 1847, fourteen houses were occupied; two were thrown down; the doors and windows were taken out of others and 12 policemen were left on the premises.[12]

The tenants next petitioned the Commissioners of Woods seeking either permission to re-occupy their holdings, or 'the means of emigration on a scale similar to that which has been lately practised by the landlords in this vicinity'.[13] The Commissioners of Woods gave their approval for assisting the evicted parties and any others who wished to emigrate, and sought the advice of the Colonial Land and Emigration Commissioners as to where they should be sent and the most efficient manner of travelling. The latter suggested that Quebec would be the best destination as there was a Government Emigration Agent there who could give advice as to the districts where employment was readily available and pay a small sum to each emigrant on arrival.[14]

The approval of the Commissioners of the Treasury was given on 12 August 1847, and on September 8, the first group of emigrants arrived in Dublin en route for Liverpool where they were to embark for New York. This party of 55, under the care of a special agent, was detained in Liverpool for several days due to the winds being contrary but sailed on the packet ship *Roscius* on 19 September 1847. A complaint from the emigrants that food was scarce was investigated and it was shown that the captain of the vessel did not issue the provisions for the voyage until she had sailed. This was the established procedure.

---

[10] *Ibid.*, 14 February 1846; Burke to Commissioners of Woods, 16 April 1846.
[11] *Ibid.*, R. Hamilton & Co., to Burke, 21 April 1846.
[12] *Ibid.*, R. Hamilton & Co., to Burke, 12 May 1847, Thomas Conry Knox, crown agent, to R. Hamilton & Co., 27 May 1847.
[13] *Ibid.*, Petition to Commissioners of Woods, 28 May 1847.
[14] *Ibid.*, Stephen Walcott, secretary Emigration Commissioners, to Charles Gore, Commissioner of Woods, 26 July 1847.

The shipping agents in charge of the arrangements were Henry and William Scott, Eden Quay, Dublin, and the charge was £4 for an adult and £2 15s. for a child under fourteen years. Provisions, tins and cooking utensils at the rate of thirty shillings each for an adult and fifteen shillings each for a child were provided, as well as landing money at the usual rate of a pound per adult and ten shillings per child, to be paid in American currency.

Between 19 September 1847 and 25 April 1848, when the last party sailed, a total of 366 persons from Ballykilcline had left Liverpool for New York, having sailed in seven different vessels. A certain consideration for the well-being of the travellers is noticeable throughout the arrangements made. Clothing was provided where necessary; a passenger too ill to sail was sent with her husband by a later vessel;[15] another 'not allowed to proceed in consequence of his great age' was transferred to Dublin and sent to New York from there.[16] By order of the Lord Lieutenant and at the request of the parish priest of Kilglass, a prisoner in the gaol of Roscommon, father of an emigrating family, was released in time to join them on the way to Liverpool.[17]

There was an increase in fares in 1848—from £4 to £4 5s. and £4 10s. (for the last party to leave) in the case of an adult, and from £2 15s. to £3 15s. for a child, with the same charge for provisions and utensils. The expenses for the emigration scheme from Bally-kilcline, by far the most comprehensive of the state-aided schemes, amounted to £2,459 14s. 3d.[18] Thus, with the exception of six families or twenty-two individuals who declined the offer to help them emigrate, and who were evicted from their holdings within a month of the departure of the last party, the entire tenantry of this estate had emigrated to America. On 17 May 1848 it was reported that the lands 'are perfectly untenanted'.

The estate was sold the following year to William George Downing Nesbitt for £5,500.[19]

---

15 *Ibid.*, Burke to Commissioners of Woods, 28 September 1847; 20 November 1847.

16 *Ibid.*, T. E. Hodder, emigration officer, Liverpool, emigration certificate; Burke to Commissioners of Woods, 21 March 1848.

17 *Ibid.*, Very Rev. Henry Brennan to Burke, 12 April 1848; Burke to Conry Knox, 15 April 1848.

18 *26th Report of Commissioners of Woods, Forests and Land Revenues*, pp. 7-8; app. no. 82, p. 104.

19 Q.R.O., Particulars of Sales of Crown Property since the year 1824, p.30. The date of the conveyance was 13 October 1849.

EMIGRANTS from BALLYKILCLINE

Itinerary : Dublin—Liverpool—New York

NAME		AGE	PERSONAL DETAILS	DATE OF DEPART- URE LIVER- POOL	DATE OF ARRIVAL NEW YORK	SHIP
Brennan,	William	70		18 Oct.	22 Nov.	*Creole*
or	Andrew	20	son	1847	1847	
Brannon	Daniel	24	son			
	Gilbert	7	son			
	Roger	28	son			
	William	26	son			
	Jane	18	daughter			
Carlon	John	30		19 Sept.	21 Oct.	*Roscius*
or	Honor	40	wife	1847	1847	
Carlin	Bridget	18 ⎫	no relationship			
	Ellen	9 ⎬	specified			
	Mary	7 ⎭				
Carrington,	John	14	with family group of James Hanly, q.v.	18 Oct. 1847	22 Nov. 1847	*Creole*
Caveney,	Luke [20]	46		25 April		*Progress*
	Mary	40	wife	1848		
	Edward	12	son			
	Luke	10	son			
	Patrick	17	son			
	Thomas	15	son			
	Anne	7	daughter			
	Catherine	1	daughter			
	Mary	19	daughter			
Cline,	William	58	father-in-law of Pat Kelly, q.v.; occupied holding	13 Mar. 1848	17 Apr. 1848	*Channing*
Colgan,	Margaret	66	occupied cabin on estate	13 Mar. 1848	17 April 1848	*Channing*
	Honor	30	daughter			
	Mary	28	daughter			
Colgan,	Patrick	44		26 Sept.	30 Oct.	*Metoka*
	Anne	40	wife	1847	1847	
	Bernard	8	son			
	Michael	4	son			
	William	1	son			
	Anne	12	daughter			
	Betty	6	daughter			
	Mary	15	daughter			
Colgan,	Patrick	36	evicted	19 Sept.	21 Oct.	*Roscius*
	Mary	40	wife	1847	1847	
	Michael	19	son			
	Patrick	8	son			
	Anne	7	daughter			
	Bridget	12	daughter			
	Margaret	16	daughter			

[20] Q.R.O., Correspondence—Ballykilcline. Released from Roscommon Jail by order of the Lord Lieutenant, 14 April 1848, at the request of the parish priest, Very Rev. H. Brennan.

Name		Age	Personal Details	Date of Depart- ure Liver- pool	Date of Arrival New York	Ship
Connor,	James	45	occupied holding	25 April 1848		*Progress*
	Honor	44	wife			
	Martin	22	son			
Connor,	John	37	evicted; did not sail with party in *Metoka* due to wife's illness; died at sea. [21]	30 Sept. 1847	19 Nov. 1847	*Jane Classon*
	Catherine	27	wife			
Connor,	Terence	50	evicted	19 Sept. 1847	21 Oct. 1847	*Roscius*
	Mary	35	wife			
	Thomas	20	son			
	Mary	11	daughter			
Costello,	Ellen	55		18 Oct. 1847	22 Nov. 1847	*Creole*
	John	8	son			
	Bridget	16	daughter			
	Mary	18	daughter			
Costello,	Thomas	46	occupied holding	13 Mar. 1848	17 April 1848	*Channing*
	Mary	45	wife			
	Martin	12	son			
	Michael	14	son			
	Pat	17	son			
	Thomas	6	son			
	Anne	16	daughter			
Croghan,	Patrick	28	evicted	19 Sept. 1847	21 Oct. 1847	*Roscius*
	John	24	brother			
	Margaret	26	sister			
Deffely, or Deffley	Mary George James	60 26 20	no relationship specified	18 Oct. 1847	22 Nov. 1847	*Creole*
Deffely, or Deffley	Patrick	60		18 Oct. 1847	22 Nov. 1847	*Creole*
	Mary	55	wife			
	Bridget	14	daughter			
Donlan, or Donnellan	Martin	32	not evicted; no family relationship specified.	19 Sept. 1847	21 Oct. 1847	*Roscius*
Donlon,	Patrick	28		18 Oct. 1847	22 Nov. 1847	*Creole*
	Anne	27	wife			
Donlan,	Patrick	60		18 Oct. 1847	22 Nov. 1847	*Creole*
	Edward	25	son			
	John	36	son			
	Patrick	27	son			
	William	16	son			
	Margaret	14	daughter			
Fallon,	Garret	32		18 Oct. 1847	22 Nov. 1847	*Creole*
	Eliza	26	wife			
	Bridget	20	sister			

[21] Q.R.O., O.W. Land Revenue Series Letter Books, Burke to Commissioners of Woods, 28 March 1848.

NAME		AGE	PERSONAL DETAILS	DATE OF DEPART-URE LIVER-POOL	DATE OF ARRIVAL NEW YORK	SHIP
Fallon,	Thomas	33		18 Oct.	22 Nov.	*Creole*
	Anne	32	wife	1847	1847	
	Martin	5	son			
	Ellen	8	daughter			
	Mary	1	daughter			
	Patrick	16	brother of Thomas			
	Bridget	25	sister of Thomas			
Falion,	Thomas	43		18 Oct.	22 Nov.	*Creole*
	Mary	18	wife	1847	1847	
Farrell,	Bridget	36	no relationship specified	13 Mar. 1848	17 April 1848	*Channing*
Farrell,	Pat	55	occupied cabin on estate; another son John, stayed in Liverpool with his grandmother.[22]	13 Mar. 1848	17 April 1848	*Channing*
	Mary	50	wife			
	William	18	son			
	Bridget	14	daughter			
	Mary	16	daughter			
Finne, or Finn	Patrick	35		26 Sept. 1847	30 Oct. 1847	*Metoka*
	Margaret	24	wife			
	Michael	22	brother of Patrick			
	Bridget	20	sister of Patrick			
	Margaret	9	sister of Patrick			
Fox,	Francis	35	lived in cabin on estate, no land	13 Mar. 1848	17 April 1848	*Channing*
	Mary	33				
	Francis	4	son			
	Pat	7	son			
	Thomas	26	brother of Francis			
	Catherine	16	sister of Francis			
Gallagher,	Michael	24		26 Sept. 1847	30 Oct. 1847	*Metoka*
	Margaret	20	sister			
Geenty, or Ginty	Margaret or Mary	60		26 Sept. 1847	30 Oct. 1847	*Metoka*
	Bernard	14	son			
	Bridget	16	daughter			
Gill,	Bernard	30	occupied cabin on estate	13 Mar. 1848	17 April 1848	*Channing*
	Catherine	25	wife			
	Andrew	3	son			
	Pat	2	son			
Hanly, or Hanley	James	64		26 Sept. 1847	30 Oct. 1847	*Metoka*
	Betty	54	wife			
	James	14	son			
	John	18	son			
	Martin	22	son			
	Patrick	20	son			
	Roger	12	son			
	Mary	17	son			

[22] Q.R.O., O.W. Land Revenue Series Letter Books, Burke to Commissioners of Woods, 21 March 1848.

NAME		AGE	PERSONAL DETAILS	DATE OF DEPART- URE LIVER- POOL	DATE OF ARRIVAL NEW YORK	SHIP
Hanly, or Hanley	James	30		18 Oct. 1847	22 Nov. 1847	*Creole*
	Susan	30	wife			
	John	7	son			
	Peter	5	son			
Hanly, or Hanley	Thomas	60		18 Oct. 1847	22 Nov. 1847	*Creole*
	Mary	50	wife			
	Darby	16	son			
	Edward	18	son			
	Michael	13	son			
	Patrick	24	son			
	Honor	22	daughter			
	Mary	20	daughter			
Hoare,	Michael	35	occupied holding	13 Mar. 1848	17 April 1848	*Channing*
	Mary	30	wife			
	James	5	son			
	John	7	son			
	Thomas	2	son			
	Bridget	8	daughter			
	Mary	11	daughter			
Kelly,	James	45	occupied holding	13 Mar. 1848	17 April 1848	*Channing*
	Mary	40	wife			
	Edward	18	son			
	James	16	son			
	John	2	son			
	Anne	12	daughter			
	Catherine	14	daughter			
	Eliza	10	daughter			
	Ellen	7	daughter			
	Mary	20	daughter			
Kelly,	Pat	40	occupied holding ; son-in-law of William Cline who sailed in *Channing*.	25 April 1848		*Progress*
	Eliza	36	wife			
	Thomas	12	son			
	William	8	son			
	Anne	10	daughter			
	Bridget	1	daughter			
	Maria	14	daughter			
McCormack, or McCormick	Catherine	55	was ill in quarantine hospital, but recovered.	26 Sept. 1847	30 Oct. 1847	*Metoka*
	Patrick	22	son			
	Peter	15	son			
	Anne	9	daughter			
	Ellen	30	daughter			
McCormick,	Edward	40		26 Sept. 1847	30 Oct. 1847	*Metoka*
	Margaret	32	wife			
	Edward	4	son			
	James	1	son			
	Thomas	8	son			
	Anne	14	no relationship specified			
	Catherine	6				
	Mary	18				
McCormick, or McCormack	Mary	26		26 Sept. 1847	30 Oct. 1847	*Metoka*
	Anne	20	sister			
	Bridget	24	sister			

NAME	AGE	PERSONAL DETAILS	DATE OF DEPART-URE LIVER-POOL	DATE OF ARRIVAL NEW YORK	SHIP
McCormick, Michael	19		18 Oct. 1847	22 Nov. 1847	*Creole*
Honor	17	sister			
Margaret	19	sister			
Sally	16	sister			
McCormick, Pat	32	occupied holding	13 Mar. 1848	17 Apr. 1848	*Channing*
Catherine	28	wife			
Michael	4	son			
Pat	6	son			
Anne	8	daughter			
Mary	20	sister of Pat			
McDermott, Hugh	50	evicted	19 Sept. 1847	21 Oct. 1847	*Roscius*
Eliza	48	wife			
Bernard	28	son			
Hugh	12	son			
James	26	son			
John	24	son			
William	18	son			
Anne	25	daughter			
Bessy	20	daughter			
Ellen	13	daughter			
Rosanna	14	daughter			
Susan	22	daughter			
McDermott, Mary	44		26 Sept. 1847	30 Oct. 1847	*Metoka*
John	13	son			
Thomas	15	son			
Bridget	11	daughter			
Ellen	20	daughter			
Mary	17	daughter			
McDermott, Michael	44		26 Sept. 1847	30 Oct. 1847	*Metoka*
Ellen	40	wife			
Michael	16	son			
Anne	8	daughter			
Betty	14	daughter			
Ellen	10	daughter			
Maria	12	daughter			
McDonnell, Andrew	18		13 Mar. 1848	17 Apr. 1848	*Channing*
Anne	22	sister			
Ellen	16	sister			
McDonnell, Michael	50	occupied cabin on estate	13 Mar. 1848	17 Apr. 1848	*Channing*
Michael	21	son			
Catherine	24	daughter			
Mary	18	daughter			
McDonnell, Patrick	24	no family relation-ship specified	26 Sept. 1847	30 Oct. 1847	*Metoka*
McGann, or McGanne John	24	occupied holding	13 Mar. 1848	17 Apr. 1848	*Channing*
Atty	19	brother			
Luke	20	brother			
Anne	26	sister			
Mary	15	sister			
John	1	no relationship specified			

NAME		AGE	PERSONAL DETAILS	DATE OF DEPART- URE LIVER- POOL	DATE OF ARRIVAL NEW YORK	SHIP
McGann,	Mary	40	occupied holding	13 Mar. 1848	17 Apr. 1848	*Channing*
or	James	18	son			
McGanne	John	5	son			
	Thomas	8	son			
	Anne	1	daughter			
	Bridget	10	daughter			
	Eliza	14	daughetr			
McManus,	Thomas	29	occupied holding	13 Mar. 1848	17 Apr. 1848	*Channing*
	James	20	brother			
McManus,	Thomas	24	occupied holding	13 Mar. 1848	17 Apr. 1848	*Channing*
	Andrew	21	brother			
	Pat	23	brother			
	Mary	18	brother			
Madden,	Mary	46	occupied cabin on estate	13 Mar. 1848	17 Apr. 1848	*Channing*
	Thomas	13	son			
	Catherine	16	daughter			
Magan,	John	34		18 Oct. 1847	22 Nov. 1847	*Creole*
	Patrick	22	brother			
	Anne	28	sister			
	Ellen	26	sister			
	Catherine	24	sister			
Maguire,	John	30		18 Oct. 1847	22 Nov. 1847	*Creole*
	Mary	30	wife			
	Patrick	5	son			
	Mary	3	daughter			
Moran,	John	56		26 Sept. 1847	30 Oct. 1847	*Metoka*
	Winifred	44	wife			
	Francis	7	son			
	John	15	son			
	Catherine	10	daughter			
Mullera,	Anne	25	occupied holding; listed as head of family but on separate sailing ticket from Pat.	13 Mar. 1848	17 Apr. 1848	*Channing*
	Pat	29	no relationship specified.			
Mullera, Mullerea or Mulere	Catherine	30	occupied holding; surrendered possession.	19 Sept. 1847	21 Oct. 1847	*Roscius*
Mullera,	James	50		18 Oct. 1847	22 Nov. 1847	*Creole*
	Bridget	50	wife			
	Denis	12	son			
	Anne	9	daughter			
	Bridget	10	daughter			
Mullera, or Mulera	James	22		26 Sept. 1847	30 Oct. 1847	*Metoka*
	Thomas	20	brother			

Name		Age	Personal Details	Date of Departure Liverpool	Date of Arrival New York	Ship
Mullera,	John	35	lived in cabin on	13 Mar.	17 Apr.	*Channing*
	Sarah	30	wife estate	1848	1848	
	Francis	6	son			
	James	4	son			
	John	8	son			
	Patrick	12	son			
	Thomas	10	son			
	Pat	25	brother of John			
Mullera,	Thomas	36	occupied holding	13 Mar.	17 Apr.	*Channing*
	Mary	30	wife	1848	1848	
	Thomas	6	son			
	Anne	2	daughter			
	Bridget	55	mother of Thomas			
Narry,	Bartholomew or Bartley	45	occupied holding; brother of Pat Narry who sailed in *Roscius*	13 Mar. 1848	17 Apr. 1848	*Channing*
	Michael	26	son			
	William	36	brother			
Narry, or Neary	Patrick	40	evicted	19 Sept.	21 Oct.	*Roscius*
	Mary	28	wife	1847	1847	
	Bridget	1	daughter			
Neary,	Mary	35		18 Oct.	22 Nov.	*Creole*
	James	3	son	1847	1847	
	Anne	7	daughter			
	John	16	brother-in-law			
	Bridget	14	sister-in-law			
	Catherine	24	sister-in-law			
O'Neal, or O'Neill	Bernard	45		26 Sept.	30 Oct.	*Metoka*
	Betty	40	wife	1847	1847	
	Bernard	13	son			
	John	16	son			
	Anne	20	daughter			
Padian,	Richard	32		19 Sept.	21 Oct.	*Roscius*
	Mary	30	wife	1847	1847	
	James	9	son			
	William	12	son			
	Bridget	10	daughter			
	Maria	6	daughter			
Quinn,	Catherine	30	ill in hospital after arrival but recovered. [23]	18 Oct. 1847	22 Nov. 1847	*Creole*
	Hugh	6	son			
	James	8	son			
	John	1	son			
	Anne	3	daughter			
	Catherine	17	no relationship specified.			

---

[23] Q.R.O., O.W. Land Revenue Series Letter Books, Burke to Commissioners of Woods, 24 February 1848; 28 March 1848.

NAME		AGE	PERSONAL DETAILS	DATE OF DEPART- URE LIVER- POOL	DATE OF ARRIVAL NEW YORK	SHIP
Reynolds, James		28	evicted ; listed as head of family	19 Sept. 1847	21 Oct. 1847	*Roscius*
	Bridget	60	mother			
	John	24	son of Bridget			
	Joseph	22	son of Bridget			
	Thomas	40	} no relationship specified.			
	Bridget	14				
	Catherine	2				
Reynolds, Michael		9	listed with family of Mary McGann, but no relationship specified.	13 Mar. 1848	17 Apr. 1848	*Channing*
Reynolds, Thomas		33		26 Sept. 1848	30 Oct. 1848	*Metoka*
	Mary	30	wife			
	Andrew	5	son			
	James	8	son			
	John	6	son			
	Thomas	2	son			
	Mary		infant daughter			
	Andrew	27	brother of Thomas			
	Bridget	60	mother of Thomas			
Stewart,	Bridget	35	no land ; lived in cabin on estate	13 Mar. 1848	17 Apr. 1848	*Channing*
	James	17	son			
	Michael	5	son			
	Bridget	14	daughter			
Stewart,	Francis	56	occupied cabin on estate; sailed from Dublin [24]	16 Mar. 1848		*Laconic*
	Anne	50	wife	13 Mar. 1848	17 Apr. 1848	*Channing*
	John	30	son			
Stuart,	George	40		18 Oct. 1847	22 Nov. 1847	*Creole*
	Bridget	32	wife			
	Charles	6	son			
	John	4	son			
	Mary	10	daughter			
Stuart,	James	63	evicted	19 Sept. 1847	21 Oct. 1847	*Roscius*
	Ellen	60	wife			
	George	20	son			
	Ellen	18	daughter			
Stuart,	John	21	not listed as head of family; possibly did not occupy holding.	18 Oct. 1847	22 Nov. 1847	*Creole*
	Bridget	17	sister			
	Catherine	15	sister			
Stuart, or Stewart	Patrick	18	evicted	19 Sept. 1847	21 Oct. 1847	*Roscius*
	Catherine	25	sister			

---

[24] *Ibid.*, 21 March 1848. Burke states that due to his 'aged appearance' he was not accepted as a passenger in Liverpool and was sent from Dublin instead. A. & W. Scott to Burke, 4 July 1848, who reported that he was ill in hospital in New York. His 'landing money' was not claimed.

NAME		AGE	PERSONAL DETAILS	DATE OF DEPART- URE LIVER- POOL	DATE OF ARRIVAL NEW YORK	SHIP
Stuart,	William	47	ill in hospital after arrival, but re-covered [25]	18 Oct. 1847	22 Nov. 1847	*Creole*
	Bridget	43	wife			
	Charles	14	son			
	Michael	12	son			
	William	8	son			
	Eliza	10	daughter			
Winters, or Winter	Honor	60		26 Sept. 1847	30 Oct. 1847	*Metoka*
	Thomas	30	son			
	Honor	18	daughter			
	Margaret	24	daughter			
	Catherine	1	no relationship. specified.			
Wynne,	Bridget	30	her family had gone in *Metoka*; she had been in England at the time. [26]	13 Mar. 1848	17 Apr. 1848	*Channing*
Wynne, or Winn	John	52		26 Sept. 1847	30 Oct. 1847	*Metoka*
	Patrick	22	son			
	Mary	13	daughter			
Wynne,	Michael	60	occupied cabin on estate.	13 Mar. 1848	17 Apr. 1848	*Channing*
	Bell	55	wife			
	James	16	son			
	Catherine	13	daughter			
	Mary	18	daughter			

[25] See note 23.

[26] Q.R.O., O.W. Land Revenue Series Letter Books, Burke to George Knox, 17 February 1848.

NOTE.—The dates of arrival have been verified in files of *The Mercantile Gazette* in the British Museum Newspaper Library, which also supplied the names of the ships' masters. Eldridge commanded the *Roscius*; McGuire, the *Metoka*; Huttleston, the *Channing* and Rattoone, the *Creole*.

NOTE ON THE EMIGRATION SCHEME FROM
IRVILLOUGHTER AND BOUGHILL

The crown estates of Irvilloughter and Boughill were situated within a few miles of one another near Ahascragh in Co. Galway. Irvilloughter was in the parish of Ahascragh, barony of Clonmac-nowen, while Boughill was in the parish of Taghboy, one mile from Ballyforan village and five miles from Ahascragh itself, in the barony of Killian. The emigrants from the two estates travelled together to Galway and thence to Quebec. The official in charge of the scheme was Golding Bird, collector of excise in Galway.

Boughill was the smaller of the two estates and was an island of arable and pasture land containing 111 statute acres almost completely surrounded by 320 acres of bog. According to a survey made in 1821, the arable land was exhausted by the numbers of poor people 'who hold it in small lots at an exorbitant rent'.[1] The bog was 'an inducement to a number of petty linen manufacturers to settle thereon, inasmuch as the great abundance of turbary enables them to carry on their manufacture, by which means they pay their rents'.[2] At that time 92 individuals were resident on the estate. The immediate lessee under the Crown was Nicholas D'Arcy who was the assignee of Edward Kelly, a descendant of Hugh Kelly who had forfeited the lands after 1688. He paid an annual rent of £4 12s. 3d. and received a sum of £56 17s. 4d. and 56 days labour of men and horses per annum from John Killelea and his nine 'partners'. This estate provides one of the best examples of the working of the rundale system—the 'co-partnership or holding in joint occupation' of the land, with all its attendant difficulties of cultivation and maintenance. The Commissioners of Woods resumed possession of the estate from 4 September 1830, and granted a lease for seven years from 1831 at £50 a year to John Killelea and 'partners'.[3]

The Boughill tenants enjoyed the reputation of being 'a happy contented people', ready to pay their rent at the appointed time

---

[1] Q.R.O., Files of Forfeiture Office and Miscellaneous Papers, File No. 10; Valuation of lands of Boughill, 13 June 1821; Correspondence—Irvilloughter and Boughill, Report of Commissioners appointed to inquire into the crown's title, 23 September 1822.

[2] *Ibid.*

[3] Q.R.O., Correspondence—Irvilloughter and Boughill, Commisioners of Woods to Nicholas D'Arcy, 4 September 1830; *Ibid.* to John Killelea, 19 April 1831.

and anxious for separate leases for 21 years.[4] In a memorial for relief after 'the failure of the potatoe crop in Ireland', they asked that drainage works be started and that a passage from the public road to the estate be repaired. Michael Boyan, superintendant of Kingwilliamstown model farm, sent by the Commissioners of Woods to survey the estate, reported that their potatoes were all gone—the report was dated 28 October 1846—and that they were living on oatmeal made from the oats with which they used to pay their rents. There were 111 persons then living on the estate and he recommended that relief works to the value of £192 be started to provide food for the tenants for six months and then that 'the property should be divided into new allotments'.[5] Another survey was made of the estate in October, 1847, when, unlike most other relief schemes, it was found that careful drainage had made a considerable improvement in land hitherto unproductive. State-aided emigration was recommended for those anxious to leave as this would enable the Commissioners of Woods to enlarge the farms of those who remained behind. Furthermore, the estate would be improved fully 'to the extent of the outlay necessary' for such a scheme, 'unlike the Irvilloughter estate'.[6] In 1846 the estate was held in common between seventeen families. Each partner held between three and seven acres in several lots in different parts of the property. It may be noted that the tenants of Boughill thanked the Commissioners of Woods for the public works to which they attributed 'their exemption from the awful fate of so many of their countrymen'.[7]

The estate of Irvilloughter had been let on a sixty-one year lease from 1 May 1773 to Ross Mahon of Castlegar, Co. Galway.[8] Under the provisions of the Land Revenue Act of 1827,[9] an order of 30 October 1830, addressed to Sir Ross, determined the existing lease and the crown resumed possession. It was found that a 'numerous tenantry' was resident on the estate and the suggestion was made by James Weale, agent of the Commissioners of Woods, that a vessel be chartered to send them to America. The tenants refused the offer to help them emigrate.[10]

Sir Ross Mahon was a resident and improving landlord who had given extensive employment to the labourers of the district on his estate ; he had 'set out Irvilloughter several years since in lots

---

[4] Q.R.O., O.W. Land Revenue Series Letter Books, Norman Ashe, collector of excise, to Burke, 26 May 1845; Memorial of Boughill Tenants, 20 May 1845.
[5] *Ibid.*, Boyan to Commissioners of Woods, 28 October 1846.
[6] *Ibid.*, C.P. Brassington, surveyor, to Burke, 19 October 1847.
[7] Q.R.O., Files of Forfeiture Office and Miscellaneous Papers, File No. 12.
[8] Later Sir Ross Mahon, 1st Baronet.
[9] 7 and 8 Geo IV, c.68.
[10] Q.R.O., O.W. Land Revenue Series Letter Books, Boyan to Commissioners of Woods, 23 March 1846.

to his labourers'; (some of these lots were held in common by 6 or 8 families to each lot), and he accepted labour in lieu of rent.[11] After his death in 1835 the living conditions of the tenantry deteriorated, and by 1843 large arrears of rent due to the Commissioners of Woods had accumulated 'in consequence of extreme poverty—particularly as the prices for what small farmers have to dispose of, namely, pigs, corn and potatoes being particularly low'.[12] The tenants considered that the rent of twenty-five shillings per acre was excessive —the usual rent on adjoining properties of superior land was only fourteen shillings and four pence half-penny—and in June, 1843, they asked the Commissioners of Woods to reduce it. A temporary reduction of ten per cent. was allowed.[13] In 1846 there were 408 persons living on Irvilloughter; the estate of 694 acres was parcelled into nearly 300 separate divisions, held by a 100 tenants, and, in the opinion of the clerk of the Quit Rents, 'the holdings cannot be enlarged' until a considerable number of persons be removed.[14]

The tenants on Irvilloughter seem to have suffered more from the destitution arising from the famine than those on any of the other estates under review. The collector of excise from Galway who attended in November, 1845, to receive the rents, reported that at least a quarter of the potato crop was very seriously damaged. The oats lay out in the haggards unthreshed so he recommended that they should first of all attend to separating the good from the damaged potatoes, then that they should thresh the oats, hold a supply for seed and a reasonable amount to make good the deficiency of the potato crop, and sell the remainder at the high prices prevailing in order to pay the rent.[15] In March, 1846, Michael Boyan, who came to survey the conditions on the estate for the Commissioners of Woods, reported that the disease was increasing. 'I have been looking at the children on the estate employed peeling the *raw potatoes* when preparing them for dinner. They first peel off the skin, then they scoop out the black or diseased spots on all sides, as the disease inters (sic) into the potato at different depths, it has rather a curious appearance when cleared of all the black spots, and even it looks much worse boiled than raw. The people prefer to use them poun[d]ed or mashed up with salt, and milk when the milk can be procured, this dish they call "canny" or "calcannon" '. He referred to the gloomy pensive manner of the tenants and recommended that certain useful relief works be started :—(a) that an extensive tract of 100 acres of wet land be drained ; (b) that farm roads be

11 *Ibid.*
12 *Ibid.*, Norman Ashe to Burke, 12 May 1843.
13 *Ibid.*, Commissioners of Woods to Burke, 4 September 1843.
14 *Ibid.*, Burke to Commissioners of Woods, 11 December 1847.
15 *Ibid.*, Ashe to Burke, 15 November 1845.

made, and (c) that the level of a neighbouring river be lowered. He also reported that the population of the estate in March, 1846, was 208 males and 200 females and the number of men fit to work was 114. In fulfilment of a promise to pay their rent on the guarantee that public works would be started, the tenants paid £80 6s. 8d. out of a possible £96 16s. 5d. on 13 April 1846.

By the end of October, 1846, just over £59 was spent on these relief works. The wages of each man was 5s. per week. At least 70 men were totally dependent on the crown for employment so it was recommended that during the winter months old ditches be levelled and drains made.[16]   A memorial from the tenants in March, 1847, told of their miserable plight and their inability to pay their rents. Relief works continued and between June 21 and September 13 1847, a total sum of £221 5s. 10d. was spent on this estate and on Boughill, which was administered jointly with it.

In July, 1847, Charles Gore, one of the Commissioners of Woods, asked whether aided emigration from Irvilloughter and Boughill 'might not enhance the value of the lands to an extent commensurate with the expense that would be incurred'. That, replied Burke, was now purely a secondary consideration in view of the poverty and destitution existing on the estates, and he urged that four tenants with twelve children from Boughill, and twelve tenants with twenty-nine children from Irvilloughter, be provided with their passage money without delay.[17] No ultimate destination was specified ; getting the tenants away was for him the main consideration.

Instructions to proceed with the scheme did not come from the Commissioners of Woods until 15 December 1847, when Golding Bird was appointed to carry it out. He reported that so many of the tenants were in abject poverty that it would be necessary to supply clothing for them. The cost, estimated at £1,837 12s. 6d. for removing 223 persons, (136 adults and 87 children), was considered excessive by the Commissioners of Woods in view of the fact that upwards of £600 had been spent already on relief works on the estates. The sanction of the Treasury was not forthcoming until 29 March 1848, when £1,850 was advanced.

It was proposed by Golding Bird that the emigrants from these estates be sent from Galway. There was, he said, an 'emigrant officer' at that port as laid down by act of parliament, whose duty it was to inspect the vessels, and he guaranteed that the ships would sail punctually.   Arthur Ireland, shipping agent, Galway, quoted

---

[16] Ibid., Boyan to Commissioners of Woods, 29 October 1846.
[17] Ibid., Burke to Commissioners of Woods, 15 July 1847.

£5 6s. as the fare for an adult passenger from Galway to Quebec, and £2 15s. 6d., the fare for a child. He would supply :

2 lbs. of meal or biscuit each per day.

2 lbs. of beef or pork each per week.

1 lb. of butter each per week.

1 lb. of tea each per voyage.

9 lbs. of sugar each per voyage.

Cooking utensils also would be provided. Children under 14 would receive half the above amounts with the exception of meal when they were to receive 1½ pounds.[18]   On 25 April 1848, Burke authorised the immediate start of the project. Landing money was to be paid to the emigrants in Quebec by the emigration agent there.

The first party of 253 emigrants left Galway on 10 June 1848 on board the *Sea Bird* under Captain McDonagh, Galway, and arrived in Quebec on 23 July 1848. There were only two deaths on the voyage, (one adult and one child), a fact which was considered worthy of favourable comment by the organiser of the project.[19]   According to a report from the emigration department in Quebec, they 'all proceeded to Upper Canada with the exception of 2 families who had friends in the States'.[20]   It may be noted that in the event of the death of a passenger at sea, landing money was paid to the deceased's relatives.

The cost of the project was £1,646 9s. 11d., almost £200 less than the estimate. The population of Irvilloughter in June, 1848, was 463, so that about 220 still remained on the estate, while 73 out of a total of 104 remained in Boughill. A further scheme was expected during the spring of 1849 and petitions from the tenants praying to be sent to Canada were numerous.

On 14 July 1849, the Treasury authorised a further grant of £1,400 and Golding Bird was appointed once more to carry out the scheme. On 17 August 1849, the *Northumberland* sailed from Galway carrying 114 adults and 44 children. The shipping agents were Messrs. Evans and Sons, Galway.   Their rates were £5 7s. 6d. for an adult and £2 17s. 6d. for a child. Arrangements were made in this instance for the captain of the ship to pay head money to the port authorities at Quebec at the rate of 7s. 6d. per adult, and 5s. per child between the age of five and fifteen years. A doctor was summoned to examine the emigrants before they sailed.[21]   The *Northumberland* arrived in Quebec on 2 October 1849, after which the emigrants went by steamer to Montreal, at a reduced rate of a shilling sterling each.[22]

---

[18] *Ibid.*, Arthur Ireland to Golding Bird, 11 April 1848.

[19] *Ibid.*, Bird to Burke, 24 August 1848.

[20] Q.R.O., Files of Forfeiture Office and Miscellaneous Papers, File No. 16., A.C. Buchanan, Emigration Dept., Quebec, to Stephen Walcott, secretary, Colonial Land & Emigration Commissioners, London, 26 August 1848.

[21] *Ibid.*, File No. 18, Bird to Burke, 11 December, 1849.

[22] *Ibid.*, Buchanan to Walcott, 5 October 1849.

Four deaths occurred on the sea voyage.

The expenses amounted to £1,168 8s. 5d., making a total of £2,814 18s. 4d., for the entire project.

In 1851, about 180 persons were living on the lands but no further emigration schemes were mooted. Finally, in July, 1855, the estates were sold when Boughill realized £1,500 and Irvilloughter, £6,325.[23]

[The rentals, census and other documents to be found in Files 10 to 23 of the Files of the Forfeiture Office and Miscellaneous Papers, have been used to supplement the biographical details in the compilation of the list of emigrants from Irvilloughter and Boughill.]

---

[23] Q.R.O., Particulars of Sales of Crown Property since the year 1824, p. 23.

IRVILLOUGHTER and BOUGHILL

Name	Age	Personal Details	Date of Departure Galway	Date of Arrival Quebec	Ship
Brien, Michael Byrne or Bryne [24]	22	of Boughill; occupied cabin and rood of land ; single man ; very poor.	15 June 1848	23 July 1848	Sea Bird, Galway
Byrne, Anne	20	of Boughill; grouped with John Killalea but no relationship specified.	15 June 1848	23 July 1848	Sea Bird, Galway
Byrne, Mary	20	of Irvilloughter ; grouped with Catherine Kelly and Mary Kennedy.	17 Aug. 1849	2 Oct. 1849	Northumberland, Galway
Byrne, Michael or Birne	41	of Boughill; weaver; son of Thady, 'in a dying state' aged 90.	17 Aug. 1849	2 Oct. 1849	Northumberland, Galway.
Bridget	38	wife			
John	8	son			
Michael	11	son			
Timothy	4	son			
Ellen	18	daughter			
Byrne, Pat	15	of Boughill	17 Aug. 1849	2 Oct. 1849	Northumberland, Galway
Bridget	26	sister			
Byrne, Thomas [25]	21	of Boughill; occupied cabin only; very poor.	17 Aug. 1849	2 Oct. 1849	Northumberland,
Ellen	20	sister			
Mary	19	sister			Galway.
Carney, Anne [26]	20	of Irvilloughter; niece of John White (Red); cousin of Pat White, q.v.	15 June 1848	23 July 1848	Sea Bird, Galway
Carroll, Thomas	31	of Irvilloughter; son of Patrick and Bridget.	17 Aug. 1894	2 Oct. 1849	Northumberland, Galway.
Bridget	23	wife			
John	22	brother of Thomas			
Michael	24	brother of Thomas			
Bridget	15	sister of Thomas			
Mary Ann	18	sister of Thomas			
Ann Rafferty	20 ⎫	no relationship specified			
Mary	? ⎭				

---

[24] Writer of letter No. 4.

[25] Q.R.O., Files of Forfeiture Office and Miscellaneous Papers, File No. 15. A list in this file states that the family group of Thomas Byrne consisted of Catherine and Judith Hamberry and Mary Byrne, and stated that this family, 'Brother and Sisters, and Sister-in-law, holds only a Cabin, all wretchedly poor'. In File No. 11 it is stated that Mary Byrne was Thomas's sister and Catherine 'Amberry' his aunt.

[26] Q.R.O., Correspondence—Irvilloughter and Boughill, Census of 1836.

NAME		AGE	PERSONAL DETAILS	DATE OF DEPART- URE LIVER- POOL	DATE OF ARRIVAL NEW YORK	SHIP
Carty, or McCarthy	John	60	of Irvilloughter; occupied cottage and 3 acres; very poor.	15 June 1848	23 July 1848	*Sea Bird.* *Galway.*
	Bridget	55	wife			
	Edward	12	son			
	Martin	15	son			
	Peter	10	son			
	Thomas	14	son			
	Mary	25	daughter [27]			
	Peggy	21	daughter			
	Ann	2	no relationship specified			
Carty,	Owen	22	of Irvilloughter	17 Aug. 1849	2 Oct. 1849	*Northum- berland, Galway.*
	Catherine	20	sister			
Casey,	John	16	of Irvilloughter ; two orphans included in Denis Grady's family group.	15 June 1848	23 July 1848	*Sea Bird, Galway.*
	Pat	15				
Coffey,	Michael	20	of Irvilloughter ; included in family group of Catherine Donnellan but no relationship specified	15 June 1848	23 July 1848	*Sea Bird, Galway.*
Conway,	Bridget	42	of Irvilloughter	15 June 1848	23 July 1848	*Sea Bird, Galway.*
	Pat	16	son			
	Mary	12	daughter			
Conway,	James	27	of Irvilloughter ; occupied cabin and 1 acre; very poor.	15 June 1848	23 July 1848	*Sea Bird, Galway.*
	Margaret or Mary	24	wife, daughter of Pat Lynskey, decd.; sister of Bridget, q.v.			
	Thomas	7	son			
	Pat	2	son			
	Margaret	3	daughter			
Conway,	John	31	of Irvilloughter	17 Aug. 1849	2 Oct. 1849	*Northum- berland, Galway.*
	Biddy	20	sister			
	Catherine	36	sister			
	Mary	25	sister			
	Mary Ann	41	sister			
Cosgrave,	Bridget	50	of Irvilloughter ; widow of John ; occupied cottage and 4 acres; very poor.	15 June 1848	23 July 1848	*Sea Bird, Galway.*
	James	13	son			
	John	26	son			
	Michael	16	son			
	Pat	7	son			
	Peter	29	son			
	Thomas	20	son			
	Anne	18	daughter			
	Margaret	17	daughter			
	Mary	10	daughter			

---

[27] Q.R.O., Files of Forfeiture Office and Miscellaneous Papers, File No. 14. Mary is described here as a step-daughter of John Carty.

NAME	AGE	PERSONAL DETAILS	DATE OF DEPARTURE LIVERPOOL	DATE OF ARRIVAL NEW YORK	SHIP
Cosgrave, Ellen	24	of Irvilloughter; niece of Michael Kennedy who did not emigrate; [28] in family group of John Guinnessy but no relationship specified.	17 Aug. 1849	2 Oct. 1849	*Northumberland*, *Galway*.
Cosgrave, James	41	of Irvilloughter; son of Thomas, a thatcher, and Mary Cosgrave; occupied cabin and 1½ acres; very poor.	15 June 1848	23 July 1848	*Sea Bird*, *Galway*.
Mary	37	wife			
Pat	6	son			
Thomas	3	son			
William	2½	son			
Catherine	2	daughter			
Maria	8	daughter			
Anne	12	sister of James.			
Bridget	22	sister of James.			
Cosgrave, John [29]	24	of Irvilloughter; occupied a cottage and 1½ acres; very poor.	15 June 1848	23 July 1848	*Sea Bird*. *Galway*.
Francis	20	brother			
Ann	34	sister			
James	1	son of Ann			
John	4	son of Ann			
Thomas	11	son of Ann			
Bridget	12	daughter of Ann			
Cosgrave, Julia	22	of Irvilloughter; occupied house and 1 acre with Catherine Jennings [30] and Mary Dowd.	15 June 1848	23 July 1848	*Sea Bird*, *Galway*.
Cosgrave, Pat	35	of Irvilloughter; mason; son of Peter and Catherine; occupied a cabin and rood; very poor.	15 June 1848	23 July 1848	*Sea Bird*, *Galway*.
Mary	32	wife			
John	4	son			
Bridget	3	daughter			
Cosgrave, Thomas	38	of Irvilloughter; 'taylor'; occupied a cabin and rood; very poor.	15 June 1848	23 July 1848	*Sea Bird*, *Galway*.
Hannah	23	wife			
Hannah	1½	daughter			

[28] Q.R.O., Correspondence—Irvilloughter and Boughill, Census of 1836.

[29] Q.R.O., Files of Forfeiture Office and Miscellaneous Papers, File No. 14.

[30] In the Census of 1836, Catherine is described as a visitor to house of Thomas Cosgrave, father of James, q.v. and Judy.

NAME		AGE	PERSONAL DETAILS	DATE OF DEPART- URE LIVER- POOL	DATE OF ARRIVAL NEW YORK	SHIP
Cosgrave,	William	21	of Irvilloughter;	17 Aug.	2 Oct.	*Northum-*
	Ellen	19	sister	1849	1849	*berland,*
						Galway.
Craughwell,	Michael	20	of Irvilloughter;	17 Aug.	2 Oct.	*Northum-*
or			son of Matt & Bridget	1849	1849	*berland,*
Croghell	Ann	22	sister			*Galway.*
	Ellen	16	sister			
Craughwell,	Nancy	41	of Irvilloughter;	17 Aug.	2 Oct.	*Northum-*
			widow of Pat.	1849	1849	*berland,*
	Pat	20	son			*Galway.*
	Margaret	17	daughter			
	Peggy					
	Kenedy	40	sister of Nancy			
	John	15	son of Peggy			
	Thomas	7	son of Peggy			
Craughwell,	Peter	40	of Irvilloughter;	15 June	23 July	*Sea Bird,*
			son of Rosy; occ-	1848	1848	*Galway.*
			upied cabin and 1½			
			acres; very poor.			
	Winifred	36	wife			
	John	4	son			
	Patrick	6	son			
	Bridget	14	daughter			
	Catherine	18	daughter			
	Ellen	11	daughter			
	Kitty	20	daughter			
	Mary	16	daughter			
	Rose	13	daughter			
Craughwell,	Thomas	20	of Irvilloughter;	15 June	23 July	*Sea Bird,*
			son of Pat, decd.	1848	1848	*Galway.*
	Pat	15	brother			
	Honoria	18	sister			
	Mary	16	sister			
Curley,	Margaret	30	of Irvilloughter;	17 Aug.	2 Oct.	*Northum-*
			widow of John, son	1849	1849	*berland,*
			of Margaret.			*Galway.*
	Biddy	5	daughter			
Daw,	Thomas	32	of Irvilloughter;	15 June	23 July	*Sea Bird,*
or			occupied a cabin	1848	1848	*Galway.*
Dawe			only; very poor.			
	Bridget	28	wife			
	Pat	2	son			
	Biddy	4	daughter			
	Mary Ann	½	daughter			
	James	20	brother of Thomas			
	John	18	brother of Thomas			
	Anne	20	sister of Thomas			
	Mary	16	sister of Thomas			

NAME		AGE	PERSONAL DETAILS	DATE OF DEPARTURE LIVERPOOL	DATE OF ARRIVAL NEW YORK	SHIP
Dempsey,	Henry	50	of Irvilloughter; labourer, occupied a cabin and ½ acre. 'In a horrid state of poverty'.	15 June 1848	23 July 1848	Sea Bird, Galway.
	Catherine	47	wife			
	Henry	4	son			
	John	13	son			
	Michael	10	son			
	Patrick	21	son			
	Anne	13	daughter			
	Catherine	1½	daughter			
	Margaret	18	daughter			
	Mary	15	daughter			
Dempsey,	John	57	of Irvilloughter; occupied cottage and 1½ acres; very poor. 'An industrious quiet man'. [31]	15 June 1848	23 July 1848	Sea Bird, Galway
	Bridget	55	wife			
	John	30	son			
	Biddy	30	wife of John Jr.			
	Ann	5	daughter of John Jr.			
	Catherine	1	daughter of John Jr.			
	Margaret	6	daughter of John Jr.			
Dempsey,	Michael	32	of Irvilloughter; occupied cabin and 4 acres; very poor.	15 June 1848	23 July 1848	Sea Bird, Galway.
	Catherine	31	wife			
	Pat	5	son			
	Bridget	8	daughter			
Dolan,	Bryan	17	of Irvilloughter; orphans, nephews of, and reared by family of John Dempsey, q.v.[32]	15 June 1848	23 July 1848	Sea Bird, Galway.
	John	15				
Dolan,	Thomas	15	of Irvilloughter: in Denis Grady's family group, but no relationship specified.	15 June 1848	23 July 1848	Sea Bird, Galway.
Donnellan, Donolan or Donlon	Catherine	55	of Irvilloughter; widow of Patrick, labourer; occupied cabin and rood; very poor.	15 June 1848	23 July 1848	Sea Bird, Galway.
	John	26	son			
	Pat	20	son			
	Thomas	30	son			
	Bridget	17	daughter			
	Catherine	33	daughter			
Dooley,	Thomas	1	of Irvilloughter; orphan grandchild of Catherine Donnellan	15 June 1848	23 July 1848	Sea Bird, Galway.

[31] Q.R.O., Correspondence—Irvilloughter and Boughill, Census of 1836.
[32] Q.R.O., Files of Forfeiture Office and Miscellaneous Papers, File No. 15.

NAME		AGE	PERSONAL DETAILS	DATE OF DEPART- URE LIVER- POOL	DATE OF ARRIVAL NEW YORK	SHIP
Dowd,	Mary	20	of Irvilloughter; occupied house with Julia Cosgrave and Catherine Jennings.	15 June 1848	23 July 1848	*Sea Bird,* *Galway.*
Egan,	Bridget	51	of Irvilloughter; widow of John Egan; occupied cabin and 3 acres; very poor.	17 Aug. 1849	2 Oct. 1849	*Northum-* *berland,* *Galway.*
	John	18	son			
	Michael	10	son			
	Pat	14	son; died at sea. 33			
Egan,	Mary	20	of Irvilloughter; daughter of Bridget above.	15 June 1849	23 July 1848	*Sea Bird* *Galway.*
Flannery, or Flanary	Nicholas	40	of Irvilloughter; son of Catherine; occupied a cottage and 6 acres; very poor.	15 June 1848	23 July 1848	*Sea Bird* *Galway.*
	Nancy	38	wife			
	John	½	son; died at sea. 34			
	Michael	12	son			
	Pat	13	son			
	Catherine	8	daughter			
	Ellen	5	daughter			
	Margaret	7	daughter			
	Mary	10	daughter			
	Winifred	4	daughter			
Foster,	John	20	of Irvilloughter; an orphan reared by family of Michael Lynskey, q.v.	15 June 1848	23 July 1848	*Sea Bird* *Galway.*
Glynn,	Michael	55	of Irvilloughter;	17 Aug. 1489	2 Oct. 1849	*Northum-* *erland,* *Galway.*
	Julia	53	wife			
	Michael	21	son			
	Pat	16	son			
	Timothy	8	son			
	Bridget	26	daughter			
	Margaret	19	daughter			
	Mary	24	daughter			
	Peggy Leonard	23	no relationship speci-fied to Glynns, but niece of Patrick Leonard who did not emigrate.			
Golden,	Michael	24	of Irvilloughter; brother-in-law of Denis Grady.	15 June 1848	23 July 1848	*Sea Bird,* *Galway.*
	Hannah	24	wife, nee Grady			
	Thomas	1	son			
	Mary	3	daughter			

33 *Ibid.,* File No. 18, Burke to Bird, 1 November 1849.
34 Q.R.O., O.W. Land Revenue Series Letter Books, 10, ii, 153, Immigrant List from Quebec.

NAME		AGE	PERSONAL DETAILS	DATE OF DEPART- URE LIVER- POOL	DATE OF ARRIVAL NEW YORK	SHIP
Gormally,	Margaret	37	of Boughill; daughter of Catherine and sister-in-law of Mary Gormally, q.v.	15 June 1848	23 July 1848	Sea Bird, Galway.
Gormally or Gormley	Mary	36	of Boughill; wife of Thady; occupied cabin and 1½ acres; labourers. 'Almost naked'.	15 June 1848	23 July 1848	Sea Bird, Galway.
	John	13	son			
	Thady	4	son			
	Bridget	11	daughter			
	Catherine	9	daughter			
Grady, or Gready	Denis	30	of Irvilloughter; son of John; occupied a cottage and 8 acres; very poor; brother-in-law of Michael Golden.	15 June 1848	23 July 1848	Sea Bird. Galway.
	John	21	brother			
	Honoria	20	sister			
Grady, or Gready	Peter	31	of Irvilloughter; son of Peter and Bridget; brother of Thomas, q.v. [35]	17 Aug. 1849	2 Oct. 1849	Northum- erland, Galway.
	Mary	27	wife; daughter of John White 'Red', and sister of Pat q.v.			
	Thomas	½	son; died at sea. [36]			
	Catherine	2	daughter; died at sea.			
Grady, or Gready	Thomas	41	of Irvilloughter; son of Peter and Bridget.	17 Aug. 1849	2 Oct. 1849	Northum- berland, Galway.
	Catherine	36	wife			
	John	14	son			
	Michael	3 mths.	son			
	Pat	6	son			
	Thomas	2	son			
	Ann	11	daughter			
	Bridget	4	daughter			
Gready,	Mary	18	of Irvilloughter; included in Denis Grady's family group q.v., but no relationship specified.	15 June 1848	23 July 1848	Sea Bird, Galway.
Guinnessy,	John	27	of Irvilloughter	17 Aug. 1849	2 Oct. 1849	Northum- berland, Galway.
	Hanora	25	wife			
	John	2	son			
	Thomas	3 mths.	son			

---

[35] See Pat Mannion, p. 365. Families of Peter and Thomas shared house.
[36] Q.R.O., Files of Forfeiture Office and Miscellaneous papers, File No. 18.

NAME		AGE	PERSONAL DETAILS	DATE OF DEPART- URE LIVER- POOL	DATE OF ARRIVAL NEW YORK	SHIP
Guinnessy,	Pat	55	of Irvilloughter; carpenter.	17 Aug. 1849	2 Oct. 1849	*Northum- berland,* Galway.
	Mary	51	wife; daughter of Lackey or Laughlin Looby or Luby.			
	James	20	son			
	Malachy	16	son			
	Pat	13	son			
	Ann	14	daughter			
	Catherine	3	daughter			
Guinnessy,	Thomas	22	of Irvilloughter	15 June 1848	23 July 1848	*Sea Bird,* Galway.
	Bridget	20	sister			
Hanbury, Hambury or Hamberry	Catherine	36	of Boughill	17 Aug. 1849	2 Oct. 1949	*Northum berland,* Galway.
Hambury, or Hansbury	Judy	23	of Boughill; wife of Thomas; sister of Thomas Byrne, q.v. Travelled in family group of Darby Killalea.	15 June 1848	23 July 1848	*Sea Bird,* Galway.
Hart,	Michael	36	of Irvilloughter; son of John and Catherine, decd.	17 Aug. 1849	2 Oct. 1849	*Northum- berland,* Galway.
	Pat	2	son			
	Mary	8	daughter			
	Catherine	32	widowed sister			
	James	23	} no relationship specified.			
	John	1				
	Michael	17				
	Thomas	16				
	Catherine	14				
Horan,	Michael	38	of Irvilloughter	15 June 1848	23 July 1848	*Sea Bird,* Galway.
	Anne	34	wife			
	Michael	6	son			
	Thomas	2	son			
	Catherine	4	daughter			
	Eliza	16	no relationship specified			
Jennings,	Catherine	19	of Irvilloughter; grand-daughter of Thomas and Mary Cosgrave; occupied house with Julia Cosgrave and Mary Dowd.	15 June 1848	23 July 1848	*Sea Bird,* Galway.
Kelly,	Bryan	21	of Irvilloughter; in family group of John Rafferty, q.v.	15 June 1848	23 July 1848	*Sea Bird,* Galway.
Kelly,	Catherine	21	of Irvilloughter; with Mary Byrne and Mary Kennedy	17 Aug. 1849	2 Oct. 1849	*Northum- berland,* Galway.

NAME		AGE	PERSONAL DETAILS	DATE OF DEPART- URE LIVER- POOL	DATE OF ARRIVAL NEW YORK	SHIP
Kelly,	John (Sen.)	52	of Irvilloughter; husband of Ellen, decd.	17 Aug. 1849	2 Oct. 1849	Northum- berland. Galway.
	Barney	21	son			
	John (Jnr.)	24	son			
	Michael	18	son			
	Thomas	19	son			
	Ann	17	daughter			
	Bridget	8	daughter			
	Mary	11	daughter			
Kelly,	Margaret	35	of Irvilloughter; widow of Pat.	17 Aug. 1849	2 Oct. 1849	Northum- berland, Galway.
	Catherine	9	daughter			
	Margaret	7	daughter			
	Mary Connolly	18	no relationship specified.			
Kennedy,	Mary	24	of Irvilloughter; with Catherine Kelly and Mary Byrne.	17 Aug. 1849	2 Oct. 1849	Northum- berland, Galway.
Kennedy,	Pat	28	of Irvilloughter; died on voyage; [37] son-in-law of John Carty, q.v.	15 June 1848	23 July 1848	Sea Bird, Galway.
	Anne	24	wife			
	Bridget	24	sister			
	Catherine	19	sister			
	Pat	10	no relationship specified.			
Kennedy,	Pat (John)	48	of Irvilloughter; son of John, decd.; occupied cottage and 3 acres; very poor.	15 June 1848	23 July 1848	Sea Bird, Galway.
	Mary	40	wife			
	John	16	son			
	Thomas	6	son			
	Ann	14	daughter			
	Biddy	16	daughter			
	Bridget	20	daughter			
	Catherine	18	daughter			
	Hannah	12	daughter			
	Mary	10	daughter			
	Peggy	4	daughter			
Kennedy,	Thomas	30	of Irvilloughter; son of Patrick (Marks) and Mary.	17 Aug. 1849	2 Oct. 1849	Northum- berland, Galway.
	Biddy	20	sister			
	Honoria	18	sister			
	Peggy	17	sister			
	Ellen	3	no relationship specified.			

---

[37] Q.R.O., O.W. Land Revenue Series Letter Books, Commissioners of Woods to Burke, 9 October 1848.

NAME		AGE	PERSONAL DETAILS	DATE OF DEPART-URE LIVER-POOL	DATE OF ARRIVAL NEW YORK	SHIP
Kennedy,		33	of Irvilloughter; widow of Andrew.	17 Aug. 1849	2 Oct. 1949	*Northum-berland*, Galway.
	Daniel	18	no relationship			
	Michael	17	specified.			
	Pat	12	do.			
	Ann	15	do.			
	Bridget	9	do.			
	Catherine	9	do.			
	Mary Ann	6	do.			
Kilcannon,	Anthony	17	of Boughill; in family group of Bridget Killalea, q.v.	15 June 1848	23 July 1848	*Sea Bird.* Galway.
Killalea,	Abegail	27	of Boughill; occupied cabin and 2½ acres; very poor.	17 Aug. 1849	2 Oct. 1849	*Northum-berland*, Galway.
	Biddy	25	sister			
	Catherine	20	sister			
	Ellen	17	sister			
Killalea,	Bridget	35	of Boughill ; widow of Thomas; occupied cabin and 2½ acres; very poor.	15 June 1848	23 July 1848	*Sea Bird,* Galway.
	John	8	son			
	Mark	1	son			
	Margaret	7	daughter			
	Mary	11	daughter			
Killalea,	Bridget	16	born and reared on Boughill; [38] cousin of Bridget Killalea, q.v.	15 June 1848	23 July 1848	*Sea Bird,* Galway.
Killalea,	Catherine	45	of Boughill	17 Aug. 1849	2 Oct. 1849	*Northum-berland*, Galway.
	Ann	20	daughter			
	Catherine	7	daughter			
	Margaret	15	daughter			
Killalea,	Darby	46	of Boughill; labourer.	15 June 1848	23 July 1848	*Sea Bird,* Galway.
	Margaret	44	wife			
	John	15	son			
	Bridget	9	daughter			
	Mary	16	daughter			
Killalea,	John	19	of Boughill ; grouped with Anne Byrne.	15 June 1848	23 July 1848	*Sea Bird,* Galway.
Killalea,	Mathias	45	of Boughill; labourer.	15 June 1848	23 July 1848	*Sea Bird,* Galway.
	Sally	40	wife			
	Lawrence	8	son			
	Mathias	10	son			
	Michael	19	son			
	Thomas	14	son			
	Peggy	16	daughter			
Killalea,	Patrick Senior	42	of Boughill; labourer in family group of Darby Killalea, q.v.	15 June 1848	23 July 1848	*Sea Bird,* Galway.
	Patrick	17	son			

[38] Q.R.O., Files of Forfeiture Office and Miscellaneous Papers, File No. 15.

NAME		AGE	PERSONAL DETAILS	DATE OF DEPART- URE LIVER- POOL	DATE OF ARRIVAL NEW YORK	SHIP
Loftus,	Biddy	40	of Irvilloughter; wife of Thomas; occupied a cabin only. Distress ' beggars descriptions'.	15 June 1848	23 July 1848	*Sea Bird,* Galway.
	John	15	son			
	Michael	15	son			
	Thomas	6	son			
	Biddy	9	daughter			
	Ellen	3	daughter			
	Mary	22	daughter			
	Mary Ann	16	daughter			
Looby, Luby or Lubey	John	15	of Irvilloughter; grandson of Lackey, woodcutter and wife Mary; son of Tom and Peggy; first cousin of John Guinnessy. 39	17 Aug. 1849	2 Oct. 1849	*Northum- berland,* Galway.
Lynskey,	Bridget	25	of Irvilloughter; sister-in-law of James Conway, q.v. Her father was the original tenant of the holding. 40	15 June 1848	23 July 1848	*Sea Bird,* Galway.
Lynskey,	Michael	50	of Irvilloughter; occupied cabin and 1½ acres; very poor; labourer.	15 June 1848	23 July 1848	*Sea Bird,* Galway.
	Judy	40	wife			
	John	16	son			
	Thomas	21	son			
	Catherine	10	daughter			
	Mary	12	daughter			
	Timothy	40	brother			
Lynskey,	Margaret or Mary	61	of Irvilloughter; widow of John; in family group of Thomas McLoughlin, her son-in-law.	17 Aug. 1849	2 Oct. 1849	*Northum- berland* Galway.
	Mary	20	daughter			
McLoughlin,	Thomas	37	of Irvilloughter; wife; daughter of Margaret or Mary Lynskey.	17 Aug. 1849	2 Oct. 1849	*Northum- berland,* Galway.
	Ellen	35				
	Bridget	4	daughter			
	Catherine	1	daughter			

39 Q.R.O., Correspondence—Irvilloughter and Boughill, Census of 1836.
40 Q.R.O., Files of Forfeiture Office and Miscellaneous Papers, Files Nos. 14, 15.

NAME		AGE	PERSONAL DETAILS	DATE OF DEPART-URE LIVER-POOL	DATE OF ARRIVAL NEW YORK	SHIP
Manahan, Anthony or Monaghan		20	of Irvilloughter; in family group of Owen Carty but no relationship specified; nephew of Patrick Crosby, stone cutter. [41]	17 Aug. 1849	2 Oct. 1849	Northum-berland, Galway.
Manly,	Richard	48	of Irvilloughter; occupied cabin only; very poor.	15 June 1848	23 July 1848	Sea Bird, Galway.
	Bridget	40	wife			
	James	9	son			
	John	12	son			
	Richard	3	son			
	Bridget	16	daughter			
	Ellen	18	daughter			
	Mary	14	daughter			
Mannion,	Pat	38	of Irvilloughter; with family group of Peter Grady, q.v.	17 Aug. 1849	2 Oct. 1849	Northum-berland Galway.
	Peggy	40	wife; sister of Peter and Thomas Grady.			
	John	17	son			
	Malachy	10	son			
	Pat	13	son			
	Thomas	8	son			
	Mary	5	daughter			
Morrissey, John		40	of Irvilloughter; occupied cabin and ½ acre; very poor.	15 June 1848	23 July 1848	Sea Bird, Galway.
	Hannah	33	wife			
	Pat	3	son			
	Bridget	2	daughter			
	Catherine	4	daughter			
	Ellen	11	daughter			
	Maria	10	daughter			
Morrissey, Thomas (Roger)		37	of Irvilloughter; occupied cabin and 1 acre; very poor.	15 June 1848	23 July 1848	Sea Bird, Galway.
	Peggy	36	wife			
	John	12	son			
	Bridget	6	daughter			
	Mary	8	daughter			
Mullen, or Mullin	Mary	45	of Irvilloughter; widow; occupied cabin only; very poor and almost naked.	15 June 1848	23 July 1848	Sea Bird, Galway.
	John	14	son			
Naughton, Catherine		26	of Irvilloughter; in family group of Pat Cosgrave but no relationship specified.	15 June 1848	23 July 1848	Sea Bird, Galway.

---

[41] Q.R.O., Files of Forfeiture Office and Miscellaneous Papers, File No. 15.

Name		Age	Personal Details	Date of Departure Liverpool	Date of Arrival New York	Ship
Rafferty, Ellen		24	of Irvilloughter	17 Aug. 1849	2 Oct. 1849	*Northumberland*, Galway.
	Catherine	15	sister			
	Mary	20	sister			
Rafferty, Ellen C.		22	of Irvilloughter; in family group of Catherine Donnellan but no relationship specified.	15 June 1848	23 July 1848	*Sea Bird*, Galway.
Rafferty, John		50	of Irvilloughter; ' fish tramper to and from Galway'; occupied cottage and 1½ acres; very poor. [42]	15 June 1848	23 July 1848	*Sea Bird*, Galway.
	Mary Ann	50	wife			
	John	15	son			
	Pat	18	son			
	Bridget	24	daughter			
	Catherine	20	daughter			
	Mary Ann	22	daughter			
Rafferty, Mary		40	of Irvilloughter; widow of John; occupied cabin and 1½ acres; very poor.[43]	15 June 1848	23 July 1848	*Sea Bird*, Galway.
	John Jun.	20	son			
	Pat	16	son			
	Thomas	12	son			
	Catherine	15	daughter			
Spencer, Mary		13	of Irvilloughter; an orphan reared in family of Michael Lynskey, q.v.	15 June 1848	23 July 1848	*Sea Bird*, Galway.
White,	Anne	16	of Irvilloughter	15 June 1848	23 July 1848	*Sea Bird* Galway.,
White,	Bridget	36	of Irvilloughter; widow of Pat, son of Edward and Peggy; labourer.	17 Aug. 1849	2 Oct. 1849	*Northumberland*, Galway.
	John	6	son			
	Pat	16	son			
	Bridget	8	daughter			
	Margaret	10	daughter			
	Mary	16	daughter			
White,	Bridget	39	of Irvilloughter; widow of Thomas; occupied cabin and 1½ acres; very poor.	17 Aug. 1849	2 Oct. 1849	*Northumberland*, Galway.
	Ann	14	daughter			
	Catherine	6	daughter			
	Mary	15	daughter			
	Sally	19	daughter, died at sea.[44]			

[42] Q.R.O., Correspondence—Irvilloughter and Boughill, Census of 1836.
[43] Q.R.O., Files of Forfeiture Office and Miscellaneous Papers, File No. 12.
[44] *Ibid.*, File No. 18.

NAME		AGE	PERSONAL DETAILS	DATE OF DEPART-URE LIVER-POOL	DATE OF ARRIVAL NEW YORK	SHIP
White,	John 'Black'	50	of Irvilloughter; occupied cottage and 6 acres ; very poor and half naked.	15 June 1848	23 July 1848	*Sea Bird,* Galway.
	Bridget	41	wife			
	John	16	son			
	Martin	12	son			
	Michael	6	son			
	Pat	14	son			
	Biddy	15	daughter			
	Jane	3	daughter			
	Mary	20	daughter			
	Nancy	18	daughter			
White,	Michael	21	of Irvilloughter	17 Aug. 1849	2 Oct. 1849	*Northum-berland.* Galway.
	Margaret	22	sister			
White,	Pat	26	of Irvilloughter; son of John (Red) and Catherine.	15 June 1848	23 July 1848	*Sea Bird,* Galway.
	John	18	brother			
White,	Thomas	26	of Irvilloughter	17 Aug. 1849	2 Oct. 1849	*Northum-berland,* Galway.
	Honor or Harriet	28	wife; daughter of James Finnerty or Ferraghty.[45]			
	Michael	6	son			
	Bridget	3	daughter			
	Margaret	7	daughter			

---

[45] Q.R.O., Files of Forfeiture Office and Miscellaneous Papers, File No. 11.

NOTE ON THE EMIGRATION SCHEME FROM
KINGWILLIAMSTOWN

The crown estate of Kingwilliamstown was situated in the parish of Nohaval Daly, barony of Duhallow, near Kanturk and the Cork-Kerry border, in Co. Cork. The decision to promote a state-aided emigration scheme for the estate was taken by the Commissioners of Woods some time after 11 April 1849, when a report from Richard Griffith recommended such a scheme for the removal of the 'surplus population'.[1]   The crown agent on the estate, Michael Boyan, who also had charge of the model farm experiment at Kingwilliamstown, was instructed to prepare lists of those who would emigrate willingly, or whose compulsory removal was necessary for the 'improvements' on the estate.

A Treasury warrant of 6 August 1849 authorised the expenditure of £1,500 for removing 238 persons, 158 adults and 80 children, from Kingwilliamstown to New York, at an estimated cost of £6. 15s. for each adult and £5. 3s. for each child. A first instalment of £800 was sent to Boyan, with instructions to proceed with the implementation of the scheme.[2]

The first party, consisting of 119 persons, left Kingwilliamstown for Cork on 30 August 1849. They sailed for Liverpool aboard the 'Nimrod', and embarked for New York on 7 September 1849. Kennelly and Company, of 23 Maylor Street, Cork, agents of the Liverpool firm of Harnden and Company, had charge of the travel arrangements. The fare for an adult was three pounds and for a child, two pounds five shillings. Food or 'sea stores' was provided, and each adult was to receive one pound and each child ten shillings in American currency on landing in New York.[3]

Complaints by some of the Kingwilliamstown emigrants, that sufficient food was not forthcoming on the journey from Cork, were investigated by Boyan on instructions from the Commissioners of Woods. He reported that the scarcity of food was caused by the refusal of the captain of the 'Nimrod' to delay departure while supplies were being loaded.[4]   Three persons died at sea between

---

[1] Q.R.O., Correspondence—Kingwilliamstown, Richard Griffith to Commissioners of Woods, 11 April 1849. Griffith was then compiling the Ordnance Survey.

[2] Ibid., Boyan to Commissioners of Woods, 17 August 1849 ; O.W. Letter, Account, Sales, etc. entry books, Ireland, no. I 2, Commissioners of Woods to Commissioners of Treasury, 20 July 1849 ; Commissioners of Woods to Boyan, 13 August 1849.

[3] The exchange rate was $4.80 to the pound sterling. Passenger lists, invoices and receipts are to be found in Correspondence—Kingwilliamstown.

[4] Q.R.O., Correspondence—Kingwilliamstown, Boyan to Commissioners of Woods, 25 September 1849 ; T. E. Hodder, Government emigration officer, Liverpool, to Stephen Walcott, secretary Emigration Commissioners, 7 September 1849.

Cork and Liverpool and two sisters were sent home, so that only 114 persons sailed from Liverpool.[5]   The total cost of this movement of emigrants was £498. 3s. 6d.[6]

In February, 1850 a letter was delivered to the Office of Woods, having been sent from America by John Galivan or Galvin, who complained that neither he nor his family had received any provisions while in Liverpool or during the voyage to America. Reports from the emigration officer at Liverpool insisted that all the travellers had adequate supplies of food.[7]

Nevertheless, when arrangements for the departure of the second group of emigrants were being made, a copy of the tender from the shipping agents was sent by the Commissioners of Woods to the Emigration Commissioners[8] for their opinion on the amount of food to be allocated to each individual for the voyage. The fare in this instance was four pounds for an adult, three pounds ten shillings for a child under fourteen, and a pound for an infant under one year. According to the tender the food to be supplied to each adult was as follows :—

3 quarts of water daily,

2½ lbs bread or biscuit weekly,

2 lbs rice   ,,

1 ,, wheat flour   ,,

3 ,, oatmeal   ,,

½ ,, sugar   ,,

½ ,, molasses   ,,

2 ozs tea   ,,

Children under fourteen would receive half of the above quantities.[9]

In their report, the Emigration Commissioners suggested that, in order to comply with the requirements of the Passengers' Act 1849,[10] that the allowance of oatmeal be raised to five lbs weekly per person. The shipping agents should be responsible for maintaining the party in Liverpool should any delay occur before sailing.[11]

5 Ibid.
6 27th *Report of Commissioners of Woods, Forests, and Land Revenues*, app. p. 81.
7 Q.R.O., O.W. Letter, Account, Sale, etc. entry books, Ireland, no. J 2, Commissioners of Woods to Hodder, 21 February 1850 ; ibid. to Boyan, 4 March 1850.
8 Their full title was the Colonial Land and Emigration Commissioners whose chief work at this period was the regulation of emigration.
9 Q.R.O., O.W. Letter, Account, Sale, etc. entry books, Ireland, no. K 2, Commissioners of Woods to Emigration Commissioners, 29 May 1850.
10 12 & 13 *Vic.* c. 33, *sec.* 24. For an account of the emigration traffic see article by O. McDonagh in I.H.S., No. 34, pp. 162—189.
11 Q.R.O., O.W. Letter, Account, Sale, etc. entry books, Ireland, no. K 2, Commissioners of Woods to Boyan, 1 June 1850; Boyan to Commissioners of Woods, 25 May 1850.

The all-in charge of six guineas for an adult was made up of the following items :—

	£	s.	d.
Travelling expenses from Kingwilliamstown to Cork		4	0
Clothes supplied		12	0
Extra 'sea-stores'		10	0
Landing money	1	0	0
Fare and supplies	4	0	0

The all-in cost for a child was £4 16. 0. On the acceptance of the amended tender, thirty-six persons left Cork for Liverpool on 15 June 1850, and arrived at New York shortly before 29 July 1950.[12] Several of this group settled in Buffalo.

A third party of seventeen left Cork on 5 October 1850.[13] The cost of the emigration of this and the second party was £313 8s. 7d.[14]

Arrangements for the departure of the fourth and last organised party of nineteen were sanctioned by the Commissioners on 10 September 1851 and they sailed from Cork for Liverpool on 20 September.[15] Expenses amounted to £92. 19s. 3d.[16]

Thus in the three years, 1849-50-51, a total of 191 persons left Kingwilliamstown at a cost of £904. 1s. 4d., almost £600 less that the amount originally allocated for the scheme.

The population of the crown estate of Kingwilliamstown which was returned as 656, (344 males and 312 females) in the crown agent's report of 16 May 1849, had declined to 479 persons by 24 November 1852.[17] Accordingly, a scheme to send a further 100 persons to America was proposed,[18] but nothing appears to have been done and the last reference to such schemes concerns the eldest daughter of Daniel Sullivan who had been caretaker of the estate. Six pounds was advanced for her fare to America on 25 April 1855.[19]

The crown estate of more than 5000 acres which was referred to

---

[12] Q.R.O., Correspondence—Kingwilliamstown, Register of Population, 1 November 1850; Return of Expenses of Emigration for 1850, 11 December 1850.
[13] Q.R.O., *Reports on Kingwilliamstown improvements*, Richard Griffith, 5 June 1851, in Par. Paper, No. 612, Session 1854.
[14] *28th Report of Commissioners of Woods, Forests and Lands Revenue*, app. p. 141.
[15] Q.R.O., O.W. Letter, Account, Sale, etc. entry books, Ireland, no. 1 2, Commissioners of Woods to Boyan, 10 September 1851 ; Correspondence—Kingwillaimstown, Boyan to Commissioners of Woods, 17 February 1852.
[16] *29th Report of Commissioners of Woods, Forests, and Land Revenues*, app. p. 115.
[17] Q.R.O., Register of population of Kingswilliamstown, Boyan to Commissioners of Woods, 16 May 1849 ; Correspondence—Kingwilliamstown, ibid., 24 November 1852.
[18] Q.R.O., MSS reports on Kingwilliamstown, Report of S.G. MacCulloch, 31 December 1852.
[19] Q.R.O., Correspondence—Kingwilliamstown, Commissioners of Woods to Boyan, 25 April 1855.

as the 'mountain pasture of Pobble O'Keefe' in older surveys, was sold by auction in five lots in April 1855 for a total sum of £14,520.[20] The village which has grown on part of the estate has within the last few years been renamed Ballydesmond.

[20] Q.R.O., Particulars of Sales of Crown Property since the year 1824, pp. 32–3.

EMIGRANTS FROM KINGWILLIAMSTOWN ESTATE

Itinerary : Cork—Liverpool—New York

NAME		AGE	PERSONAL DETAILS	DATE OF DEPART-URE LIVER-POOL	DATE OF ARRIVAL NEW YORK	SHIP
Buckley,	Darby	51	of Tooreenclassagh; farmer.[21]	Sept. 1851		
	Mary	39	wife			
	John	2	son			
	Michael	16	son			
	Tade	18	son			
	Johanna	9	daughter			
	Margaret	5	daughter			
	Mary	12	daughter			
Casey,	John	56	of the Town Farm; wife named Rosian;[22] two of his daughters were sent back from Liverpool. One had not 'use of one leg'.[23] Mary Sullivan was of this family group.	7 Sept. 1849	22 Oct. 1849	Columbus
	Michael	13	son			
	Bab or Barbara	19	daughter			
	Johanna	18	daughter			
	Rosean	16	daughter			
Collins,	Mary	27	niece of Mary Guiney; left with Guiney family and probably went to Buffalo with them.[24]	June 1850		
Connell,	David	45	of Glencollins; probably stayed in New York	7 Sept. 1849	22 Oct. 1849	Columbus
	Margaret	35	wife			
	Dan	15	son			
	Jerry	10	son			
	John	13	son			
	Pat	3	son			
	Eileen	½	daughter			
	Johanna	8	daughter			
	Margaret	9	daughter			
	Mary	5	daughter			

[21] *Census of Ireland, 1901, General Topographical Index.* With the exception of the townland Tooreenkeagh, which is mentioned in the censuses of 1834, 1836/7, available in Q.R.O., Correspondence—Kingwilliamstown, all the townlands mentioned are listed in above. The crown lands of Pobble O'Keefe contained in addition to the village of Kingwilliamstown the following townlands: Meenganine, Carriganes, Tooreenkeagh, Glencollins, Tooreenglanahee and Tooreenclassagh.
[22] Q.R.O., Correspondence—Kingwilliamstown, Return of Population for Kingwilliamstown, April, 1849, gives Rosian's age as 54.
[23] Ibid., Michael Boyan to Commissioners of Woods, 25 September 1849.
[24] See letters herewith pp. 386-94 for this and other probable destinations of emigrants.

Name		Age	Personal Details	Date of Departure Liverpool	Date of Arrival New York	Ship
Connell,	Patrick	50	of Town Farm ; farmer.	7 Sept. 1849	22 Oct. 1849	*Columbus*
	Ellen	44	wife			
	Dan	16	son			
	John	13	son			
	Philip	19	son			
	Johanna	4	daughter			
	Judy	15	duaghter			
	Margaret	7	daughter			
	Mary	22	daughter			
Cremin,	John	28	brother of Timothy, farmer, who did not emigrate.	7 Sept. 1849	22 Oct. 1849	*Columbus*
	Kitty	25	wife			
	Timothy	3 mths.	son			
Cronin,	Betty	17	daughter of Mary Cronin, widow of John of Glencollins, who did not emigrate; went to Norfolk.	June 1850		
Daly,	Daniel	50	of Glencollins ; labourer, native of Kerry; died on the way to America.[25]	7 Sept. 1849	22 Oct. 1849	*Columbus*
	Margaret	50	wife			
	John	26	son; went to Norfolk leaving family at New York.			
	Bessy	25	daughter			
	Judy	20	daughter			
	Margaret	19	daughter			
Danihy,	Denis (Daniel)	40	of Tooreenclassagh; farmer, native of Kerry; died on the way to Liverpool from Cork;[26] wife and family went to Buffalo.	7 Sept. 1849	22 Oct. 1849	*Columbus*
	Johanna	40	wife			
	Con	15	son			
	Dan	17	son			
	Denis	7	son			
	Matt	5	son			
	Michael	13	son			
	Mary	19	daughter			
	Mary	13	niece; daughter of Michael, brother of Denis (Daniel) Sen.			

---

[25] Q.R.O., Correspondence—Kingwilliamstown, Michael Boyan to Commissioners of Woods, 25 September 1849,
[26] Ibid.

Name		Age	Personal Details	Date of Departure Liverpool	Date of Arrival New York	Ship
Danihy,	Denis (Matt)	60	of Tooreenclassagh; farmer, native of Kerry; settled with all his family in Buffalo.	7 Sept. 1849	22 Oct. 1849	*Columbus*
	Johanna	50	wife			
	Daniel	19	son			
	Denis	7	son			
	John	17	son			
	Matt	21	son			
	Michael	11	son			
	Tade	3	son			
	Bridget	15	daughter			
	Eileen	10	daughter			
	Mary	23	daughter			
Danihy,	John	25	of Tooreenglanahee; son of Ellen, aged 65 in 1850; brother Daniel did not emigrate; stayed in New York.	June 1850		
	James	21	brother, who went to Orange County, N.Y.			
	Eileen (or Ellen)	27	sister, who went to Orange County, N.Y.			
	Kitty	30	sister, who stayed in New York.			
Danihy,	Tim	40	of Glencollins; labourer.	7 Sept. 1849	22 Oct. 1849	*Columbus*
	Mary	42	wife			
	Con	3	son			
	Dan	13	son			
	Michael	8	son			
	Tade	5	son			
	Nelly	10	daughter			
Dillon,	Pat	47	overseer of labourers at Kingwilliamstown; had already sent out two daughters at own expense.[27]	June 1850		
	Judy	51	wife			
	Margaret	23	daughter			
Duggan,	Denis	27	farmer, son of Daniel of Tooreenglanahee and Mary, his wife who did not emigrate; writer of letter No. 3, p. 393; settled in Buffalo.	June 1850		

---

[27]   Q.R.O., Correspondence—Kingwilliamstown, List of emigrants.

NAME		AGE	PERSONAL DETAILS	DATE OF DEPART- URE LIVER- POOL	DATE OF ARRIVAL NEW YORK	SHIP
Duggan,	Margaret or Madge	29	daughter of Harry Duggan, farmer, of Tooreenglanahee, a blind man, and Norry, his wife who did not emigrate; went to New Jersey.	June 1850		
	Eileen or Helen	25	sister; went to Buffalo.			
Fenigan,	Daniel	55	labourer	7 Sept. 1849	22 Oct. 1849	*Columbus*
	Johanna	48	wife			
	Johanna	20	daughter			
	Judy	7	daughter			
	Kitty	10	daughter			
	Mary	22	daughter			
Foley, or Fowley	John	52	of Carriganes; farmer; native of Kerry.	7 Sept. 1849	22 Oct. 1849	*Columbus*
	Eileen	50	wife			
	Dan	18	son			
	John	21	son			
	Pat	16	son			
	Eileen	28	daughter			
	Johanna	11	daughter			
	Julea	8	daughter			
	Mary	24	daughter; died in Liverpool.[28]			
Galvin,	John	32	mason	7 Sept. 1849	22 Oct. 1849	*Columbus*
	Margaret	30	wife			
	Patrick	2	son			
	Tade	4	son			
	Biddy	6	daughter			
Galvin,	Tade	30	brother of John above.	7 Sept. 1849	22 Oct. 1849	*Columbus*
Guiney,	Darby	45	of Glencollins; labourer.	Oct. 1850		
	Kitty	37	wife			
	Ben	5	son			
	Dan	17	son			
	Darby	3	son			
	Tade	5	son; twin of Ben.			
	Biddy	9	daughter			
	Eileen	11	daughter			
	Joney	13	daughter			

---

[28]   Q.R.O., Correspondence—Kingwilliamstown, Michael Boyan to Commissioners of Woods, 25 September 1849,

NAME		AGE	PERSONAL DETAILS	DATE OF DEPARTURE LIVERPOOL	DATE OF ARRIVAL NEW YORK	SHIP
Guiney,	Mary	50	widow of Benjamin Guiney, farmer, of Glencollins; daughter of 'Big' Daniel Leary of Tooreenglanahy and Johanna, his wife; aunt of Mary Collins above; settled in Buffalo with family.	June 1850		
	Ben	8	son			
	Dan	23	son			
	Tade	14	son			
	Gubby	11	daughter			
Keeffe,	John	25	son of John Keeffe, farmer, of Tooreenclassagh and Mary his wife, who did not emigrate; settled in Buffalo.	June 1850		
	Hanora or Norry	19	sister			
Keeffe, or O'Keeffe	Margaret	50	listed among labourers	7 Sept. 1849	22 Oct. 1849	Columbus
	Eugene	17	son			
	Jeane	13	daughter			
	Johanna	21	daughter			
	Nano	23	daughter			
Kelleher,	Daniel	69	of Tooreenglanahee	7 Sept. 1849	22 Oct. 1849	Columbus
	Dan	29	son			
	Kitty	26	wife of Daniel, junior			
	Tade	2	son of Daniel, junior			
	Kitty	3	daughter of Daniel, junior			
	Mary	21	daughter of Daniel, senior			
	John	36	nephew of Daniel, senior			
Leary,	Catherine	22	daughter of Timothy Leary of Tooreenkeagh, a farmer, who did not emigrate and his late wife, Peg.	June 1850		
Leary,	Connor or Daniel	55	labourer, later farmer of Glencollins; died in hospital probably in Buffalo, shortly after landing; family settled in Buffalo.	7 Sept. 1849	22 Oct. 1849	Columbus
	Ellen	50	wife; widow by 9 Aug. 1850.			
	Jerry	11	son			
	John	18	son			
	Eileen	16	daughter			
	Johanna	20	daughter			
	Mary	13	daughter			
	Peggy	5	daughter			

NAME		AGE	PERSONAL DETAILS	DATE OF DEPART-URE LIVER-POOL	DATE OF ARRIVAL NEW YORK	SHIP
Leary,	John	19	son of late John 'Bawn' Leary, farm-er, and Kate, his wife; brother of Pat who did not emig-rate; settled in Nor-folk.	June 1850		
Leary,	Mary	22	daughter of Daniel Leary, labourer and Ellen or Peg his wife; went out to Tade Houlihan with Betty Murphy and Davy Connell.	June 1850		
Leary	Matthew	50	of Tooreenglanahee; labourer, settled in Buffalo with his family.	7 Sept. 1849	22 Oct. 1849	*Columbus*
	Mary	45	wife			
	Dan	6	son			
	Darby	18	son			
	John	16	son			
	Matt	1	son			
	Pat	13	son			
	Johanna	4	daughter			
	Judy	20	daughter			
McAuliffe,	Denis	28	of Carriganes; son of Robert, farmer, nat-ive of Newmarket.	7 Sept. 1849	22 Oct. 1849	*Columbus*
	Michael	22	brother			
	Robert	17	brother			
	Johanna	24	sister			
McCarthy,	Margaret	22	daughter of Sandy McCarthy, carpenter to the Crown estate, native of Boherboy, and Nell his wife; wrote letter of date 22 Sept. 1850, pp. 390-3; settled in New York.	7 Sept. 1849	22 Oct. 1849	*Columbus*
Minehan, or Moynihan	Biddy	41	widow, daughter of Johanna aged 74 in 1849.	Sept 1851		
	John	15	son			
	Patrick	12	son			
Moynihan, or Moynehan	Denis	33	labourer, who 'took a house in New York'.[29]	June 1850		
	Johanna	28	wife			
	John	2	son			
	Johanna	5	daughter			

[29] See p. 389.

NAME		AGE	PERSONAL DETAILS	DATE OF DEPART- URE LIVER- POOL	DATE OF ARRIVAL NEW YORK	SHIP
Mahony, or Moynehan	Mary	55	widow, included among labourers.	June 1850		
	Dan	18	son			
	Tade	14	son			
	Ellen	26	daughter			
	Johanna	21	daughter			
	Norry	12	daughter			
Murphy,	Jane	20	daughter of Michael Murphy, farmer, of Tooreenclassagh, and Mary his wife, who did not emigrate; settled in Norfolk.	June 1850		
Murphy,	Johanna	20	daughter of Timothy Murphy, farmer, of Tooreenclassagh, and Margaret or Mary, his wife, who did not emigrate; settled in New York.	June 1850		
Reen,	Darby	51	(oge) of Tooreen-glanahee.[30]	Sept. 1851		
	Bridget	41	wife			
	Jerry	9	son			
	John	12	son			
	Michael	15	son			
	Tade	19	son			
	Ellen	5	daughter			
	Mary	6	daughter			
Reen,	Denis	25	son of late Darby Reen, farmer, of Tooreenglanahee, [31] and Biddy his wife; brother of John who did not emigrate; settled in Buffalo.	June 1850		
	Tade	22	brother			
Sullivan,			eldest daughter of Daniel Sullivan, care-taker of Kingswil-liamstown Model Farm, also describe-ed as woodranger; six pounds advanced by the Treasury, 25 April 1855.[32]	Summer 1855		

---

[30] Return of Tenants of Kingwilliamstown, c. May 1849, describes him as farmer.
[31] Later census gives Tooreenclassagh.
[32] Q.R.O., Correspondence—Kingswilliamstown, Commissioners of Woods to Michael Boyan, 25 April 1855. In return of population of Kingwilliamstown, April 1849, Daniel Sullivan's family consists of : Peggy, wife, 41, Denis, son, 8, Madge, daughter, 14, Judy, daughter, 11, John, son, 4.

Name	Age	Personal Details	Date of Departure Liverpool	Date of Arrival New York	Ship
Sullivan, John	35	labourer, also called Pat in survey of Kingwilliamstown.	7 Sept. 1849	22 Oct. 1849	*Columbus*
Ellen	30	wife			
John	½	son			
Sullivan, Mary	25	step-daughter of John Casey, q.v.	7 Sept. 1849	22 Oct. 1849	*Columbus*
Sullivan, Pat	50	of Carriganos, farmer.	Oct. 1850		
Judy	43	wife			
Dan	4	son			
John	12	son			
Michael	8	son			
Pat	7	son			
Judy	1	daughter			
May	14	daughter			

NOTE ON THE EMIGRATION SCHEME
FROM CASTLEMAINE.

The crown estate of Castlemaine was situated in the parish of Kiltallagh, Co. Kerry, on the river Maine, a short distance inland from the bay of Castlemaine. The estate, known as the Constable's Acres, was one of the perquisites of the sinecure post of governor of the fort of Castlemaine, and was placed under the management of the Commissioners of Woods when the governorship was abolished from 12 August 1835, on the death of the last holder of the office.[1] Despite several searches made by orders of the Commissioners, no records could be found as to how or when the lands became attached or annexed to the office of governor,[2] and the estate, (which in 1839 consisted of about nine acres, a fishing weir and a village of thirty-one 'thatched Cabbins of the poorest description', and one small slate house),[3] was usually leased by the governor for the term of his interest in the office. In 1839 three of the houses were occupied by publicans, two by tradesmen and the rest by labourers. The village was in a 'reduced state', and no rent had been paid by the tenants from 1835, when the lease expired, to 25 March 1840.[4]

Arrangements were made about 1839 for the erection of a quay, and Michael Boyan, superintendant of the model farm experiment in Kingwilliamstown, was appointed overseer of the improvements. It was not until this time that possession of the premises was sought for the Crown, and by 31 March 1841, all but three of the properties had been recovered.

But in spite of the erection of the quay, and a new schoolhouse and dwelling houses in the village, the tenants' lot did not improve due to the lack of employment and scarcity of food, and when the Commissioners of Woods adopted a policy of state-aided emigration, Castlemaine was included in its scope.

There were at least three separate group departures from this estate, but despite an intensive search, the list for the second and largest party to leave has not been found among the papers in the Quit Rent Office collection.

The first party of emigrants left in the autumn of 1848 on a date subsequent to 4 September 1848.[5] Their departure is recorded in

---

[1] Q.R.O., Land Revenue Series Letter Books, Commissioners of Woods to Burke, 2 March 1841.
[2] Ibid., Paymaster of Civil Services to Burke, 25 March 1841; R. Hamilton & Co., Crown Solicitors, to Burke, 31 March 1841.
[3] Ibid.; Boyan to Commissioners of Woods, 26 November 1839.
[4] Ibid., 11 July 1840.
[5] Q.R.O., O.W., Letter, Account, Sale, etc. Entry Books, no. G 2, Commissioners of Woods to Boyan, 4 September 1848.

a report of 21 December 1848, but the names of heads of families only are given, when it would appear that twelve persons emigrated at a cost of £72 3s. 11d.[6]

A further scheme was proposed in June 1849, and the expenditure of £500 was authorised for removing forty-three adults and twenty-four children from Castlemaine to New York.[7] As far as can be discovered, in the absence of the official list, at least thirteen families, or sixty-three individuals, left at a cost of £279 7s. 1d. on or before 20 September 1849.[8] From a brief reference in a letter written at the time, it is evident that this party joined the emigrants from Kingwilliamstown who sailed on the *Columbus* from Liverpool for New York on 7 September 1849, 'at the same rate of charge' as those from Kingwilliamstown.[9] The names of Patrick O'Brien and John Coffey have been included in the list. According to a note made in the 'House Book' for that area, Coffey is described as 'having gone to America leaving his holding in the hands of the Crown'.[10]

The third party of eight left Cork on 20 September 1851, on the same day as nineteen emigrants from Kingwilliamstown, at a total cost of £42 3s. 2d.[11]

There are therefore only twenty-two names in the accompanying list which, with the group of sixty-three for which no names or details are available, (with the possible exceptions of John Coffey and Patrick O'Brien), gives a total of eighty-five emigrants. The total cost of the entire emigration project for Castlemaine was £393 4s. 2d.

The town, lands, tolls of two fairs and fishing rights in the river Maine, were sold for £1,120 in August 1855.[12]

---

[6] Ibid., no. I 2, Commissioners of Woods to Commissioners of Treasury, 21 December 1848; 29 June 1849; 28th *Report of Commissioners of Woods*, app. p. 141. No explanation is offered for the delay in returning this figure.

[7] Ibid., no. I 2, Commissioners of Treasury to Commissioners of Woods, 23 July 1849.

[8] Ibid., no. J 2, Commissioners of Woods to Boyan, 14 August 1849; 4 October 1849; no. K 2, 21 December 1850; Files of Forfeiture Office, Crown Lands—General, Rental for Castlemaine, 1853; 27th *Report of Commissioners of Woods*, app. p. 81.

[9] Q.R.O., Correspondence—Kingwilliamstown, Boyan to Commissioners of Woods, 25 September 1849.

[10] Q.R.O., Valuation Office Collection, House Book for Kiltallagh parish, Co. Kerry. These books were compiled c. 1826-51, in the course of work on the general valuation. See article by Margaret Griffith in *I.H.S.*, viii, No. 29.

[11] Q.R.O., Rental for Kingwilliamstown, Castlemaine and Kinsale estates, 1851-2 ; Correspondence—Kingwilliamstown, Boyan to Commissioners of Woods, 17 February 1952; O.W. Letter, Account, Sale, etc. Entry Books, no. L 2, Commissioners of Woods to Boyan, 10 September 1851; 29th *Report of Commissioners of Woods*, app. p. 115.

[12] Q.R.O., Particulars of Sales of Crown Property since the year 1824, p. 34.

EMIGRANTS FROM CASTLEMAINE

Name		Age	Personal Details	Date of Depart- ure Liver- pool	Date of Arrival New York	Ship
Coffey,	John[13]					
Daly,	Mary			24 Sept. 1851		
	?		daughter of Mary			
	?		mother of Mary			
Griffin,	Daniel			Sept. 1848		
	?		wife			
	?		son			
	?		son			
	?		son			
Hanifen,	Ulick[14]	30	son-in-law of Margaret Sullivan	24 Sept. 1851		
	Mary	31	wife			
	Dan	2	son			
	Mary	6	daughter			
McCarthy,	John		undertenant of Daniel Griffin	Sept. 1848		
	?		mother			
	?		sister			
Shea,	John[15]		son of Thomas who died 1848	Sept. 1848		
	?		brother			
	?		brother			
	?		sister			
O'Brien,	Patrick[16]			Prior to 4 Aug. 1851		
Sullivan,	Margaret	67	mother-in-law of Ulick Hanifen, above.	24 Sept. 1851		
Total		.....	.....	22 individuals		

---

[13] See introduction.

[14] Rental for Kingwilliamstown, Castlemaine and Kinsale estate, 1851-52. Q.R.O., Correspondence—Kingwilliamstown, Return of Population for Castlemaine estate, 4 August 1851.

[15] Q.R.O., O.W. Letter, Account, Sale, etc. Entry books, no. I 2, Commissioners of Woods to Commissioners of Treasury, 21 December 1848. The immediate reason of the emigration of the Griffin, McCarthy and Shea families was that their dwellings had been acquired and demolished preparatory to the erection of a National School in Castlemaine.

[16] Q.R.O., Correspondence—Kingwilliamstown, Return of Population on Castlemaine Estate, 4 August 1851.

NOTE ON THE EMIGRATION SCHEME
FROM KILCONCOUSE

The crown estate of Kilconcouse was situated in the parish of Kinnity, King's Co., and comprised 871 acres. This estate differed from Ballykilcline, Irvilloughter and Boughill in that in this case, from 1829 onwards, leases had been granted to the tenants for a twenty-one year term. The rents appeared to have been paid fairly regularly until the year 1846 when the famine intervened. In a report from the secretary of the Kinnity District relief committee, it was stated that twelve families of 68 persons were without any provisions and 'in a most precarious state'. Forty individuals were unable to work.[1] Subscriptions amounting to £35 were contributed by the Commissioners of Woods.

In April, 1847, the Commissioners authorised the collector of excise, Parsonstown, 'to give such indulgence in payment to each tenant as their circumstances may appear to require',[2] when a number of the tenants appealed for lenience.

The leases for twenty-one years expired in 1850 when an arrear of rent of £1,531 14s. 9d. had accumulated. It was then decided to remove the 'surplus population'; to redivide the land among those selected from the remaining tenants and to abandon the collection of arrears. The friction and unrest which arose from this redivision was the cause of an inquiry by a select Committee of the House of Lords into the management of the estate.[3]

Fifty-six persons left Kilconcouse at a cost of £363 19s. 8d.

---

[1] Q.R.O., O.W. Land Revenue Series Letter Books, Report of H. Tyrrell on Distress, c. 21 May 1846.
[2] Ibid., Commissioners of Woods to Burke, 8 April 1847.
[3] *Report from the Select Committee of the House of Lords . . . into the Management . . . of Kilconcouse*, etc., 1854, xxi, 3.

EMIGRANTS FROM KILCONCOUSE

Itinerary Dublin—Liverpool—New York.

NAME		AGE	PERSONAL DETAILS	DATE OF DEPART- URE LIVER- POOL	DATE OF ARRIVAL NEW YORK	SHIP
Blake,	Edward	50	no relationship specified.	11 June 1852[4]		
	James	3				
	Ann	25				
	Sarah	20				
	Sarah	1				
Dunn,	William	45				
	Ann	43	wife			
	James	8	son			
	William	6	son			
	Biddy	19	daughter			
Fitzgerald,	James	55				
	Margaret	58	wife			
	James	16	son			
	Hanoria	18	daughter			
	Margaret	19	daughter			
Fitzgerald,	John	42				
	Ellen	30	wife			
	Denis	12	son			
	Thomas	8	son			
	Margaret	10	daughter			
Horan,	Patrick	30				
	Catherine	29	wife			
	John	3	son			
	Ann	7	daughter			
	Catherine	5	daughter			
	Margaret	12	daughter			
	Mary	10	daughter			
Karney or Kearney	Patrick	45				
	Ann	37	wife			
	Joseph	11	son			
	Pat	18	son			
	Thomas	16	son			
	William	8	son			
	Ann	14	daughter			
	Mary	21	daughter			
Kenehan,	John	45				
	Mary	37	wife			
	Jeremiah	16	son			
	John	12	son			
	Matthew	18	son			
	William	6	son			
	Ann	8	daughter			

[4] All the emigrants from Kilconcouse sailed from Liverpool on 11 June 1852 with one exception, Patrick Lowry. It is therefore unnecessary to repeat date of departure with each family group.

NAME		AGE	PERSONAL DETAILS	DATE OF DEPART- URE LIVER- POOL	DATE OF ARRIVAL NEW YORK	SHIP
Kennedy,	Peter	63				
	Mary	50	wife			
Lowry[5]	Patrick	40				
	Ann	43	wife			
	John	20	son			
	Ann	12	daughter			
	Sarah	17	daughter			
Spain,	Biddy	30				
	Catherine	25	sister			
White,	Mary	38				
	James	13	son			
	John	8	son			
	Bridget	16	daughter			
	Mary	5	daughter			

---

[5] Q.R.O., Files of Forfeiture Office and Miscellaneous Papers, File No. 5, Burke to Commissioners of Woods, 3 September 1852, states that as Patrick Lowry has only one eye he was judged 'unfit for New York' and was sent to Philadelphia instead.

LETTERS HOME FROM EMIGRANTS WHO SETTLED IN
THE UNITED STATES

Three of the following letters were sent with a report dated 11 December 1850, by Michael Boyan to Charles Gore, one of the Commissioners of Woods. He reported on the latest group departure from the crown lands of Kingwilliamstown and observed :—'I am happy to state that those persons who emigrated in June and October last were all contented and well pleased, and several letters have been received from them and in general they are all employed and doing well, and some of them have remitted money to assist their parents. I send herewith some of the letters received from them, to show the Board that they are well employed at the same time this Estate is benefited by being relieved from their support'.[1] Two years later Boyan reported that £150 in letters of credit had been received by relatives in Kingwilliamstown.[2]

The fourth letter was written by an emigrant from Boughill, Co. Galway, to the crown agent in Galway who was in charge of the emigration scheme from that estate.

---

[1] Q.R.O., Correspondence—Kingwilliamstown, Boyan to Gore, 11 December 1850.

[2] Ibid., 24 November 1852.

1

Exchange Street Buffalo August 9th 1850.

Dear Mother and Brothers

We Embrace the opportunites of writing these few lines to you hoping that this Silent Messenger may find you and all our Dear friends and Beloved Neighbours in as good a state of health as this leaves us at present thanks be to God for his benefits to us all. Therefore we mean to let you know our Situation at present

We left New York 29th of July and Sailed out for Buffalo and arrived the following day in albany we left albany the same day and Came out on the Canal Boat which was dravon By horses it took us Eight days to come to Buffalo which was very expensive to us Bread and Milk was very Dear along the Canal we Could walk out any time we pleased and walk 2 or three miles and Could eat plenty apples when we had any Desire this place is full of Orchards and Woods this is a very fine Country you may be Sure that we had a fine prospect Comming out here and according as we were Coming out the Country was getting Better as for the Crops here the indian Meal is growing here like woods and the finest fields of Clover that ever wer seen and as to the Stock they are like the Cows to Home and horses and sheep are Just the same We could see fine large Stock of Cattle 40 and 50 Cows together and so on from that down to ten and twelve and 5 or six We could see six and 7 score of Sheep and 12 or 14 horses togather you may be sure that we seen great many wonders

the Yankees are the wisest Men in the world in respect of doing business we arrived here abot 5 o clock in the afternoon of yesterday 14 of us together where we were received with the greatest Kindness and respectibility By Mathew Leary and Denis Danihy as soon as we came in we made them off at once Matt Denis Danihy went and Brought a horse and took Dan Guineys luggage to the house and paid for it himself we had no other one but his But when we came to the house we could not state to you how we were treated we had Potatoes Meat Butter Bread and tea for Dinner and you

may be sure we had Drink after in Mathew Learys house   the whole
of Denis Danihys family and Denis Daniels wife and family   Connor
Learys wife and Daughter   But the poor woman is left a widow
Connor Died in hospital

I mean to let you know that we had a pleasant night they went
to the Store and brought 2 Dozen of Bottles of Small beer and
a Gallon of Gin otherwise whiskey   So that we were drinking untill
morning   if you were to see Denis Reen when Daniel Danihy Matt
Dressed him with clothes suitable for this Country you would think
him to be a Boss or Steward   so that we have scarcely words to
state to you how happy we felt at present

Dear friends if you were to see old Denis Danihy he never was
as Good in health and looks better than ever he did at home   Ye
would not beleive how fat and strong he is—And you may be Sure
he Can have plenty tobacco and told me to mention it to Tim
Murphy—and as to the girls that used to be troting on the bogs
at home to hear them talk English would be of great astonishment
to you

Dear friends we mean to let you know them that came out here
Denis and Tade Reen Tade Leary Dan Guiney and family Paddy
Sheehan John Keeffe and Sister Denis and Ellen Duggan   we have
plenty work at Six Shillings a day thats equal to 3 shillings of your
Money   we would get a Dollor a day in Diffirent places but we
would Sooner be all together   But if Dan Guiney got to Detroit
and that he might get a better Chance he will acquaint us of it

we left John and James Danihy after us in New York they would
be out with us But James had to go out to Ellen to Orange County
in York state She Being the first person that was Employed Kate
is in New York with her Brothers Madge Duggan is out in Jersey
Mary Reen went to Boston   Betty Murphy and Mary Leary went
out to Tade Houlihan with Davy Connell   Jonoah Murphy in New
York.[3]

Daniel Guiney means to forward a few lines to Patsey Leary
Patrick My Dear friend i am sorry to say that i had to part with
Johnny but still i am Glad to let you know that he is to be received
by his Cousins   when we Came to New York I wrote a letter to
John Dailey   But he wrote Back to me directly and wanted me to
go out to him   But he told me that there was no place fit for my
family but i could not go to him at present but I Expect to see him
in a short time   then Sir he stated to Me that Thomas Gnaw[?]
rote to him and stated to him if Johnny Came to his place to write

---

3 Almost two lines are crossed out here, but of these the words 'You all know
the reason why'—are decipherable. 'Jonoah Murphy in New York' is in
the same ink as that used for crossing out the two lines.

to him and that he would send him plenty money to fetch him out and said that it was Jerry that wrote to him about it Now Dear Patrick I went with him to the train to see him Secured for Norfolk Betsey Cronin and Jane Murphy were with him for Jack Daly wrote to me to have Betty Cronin go out to him if she had not got a place So this is how we all are Scattered in the Country Denis Moynahan has taken a house in New York

Dear Patrick and Uncles I Cannot say more at present until I get to Detroit But I hope you will let me know in the answer of this letter how my Grandfather and Tim Murphy and family are No more from me at present.

John Keeffe Means to have his Brother write to him as soon as posible and to let Know if his sister went to her husband to England and also to have his father and Mother Make themself easy and that as soon as he would have any thing earned that he would send them some assistance

Ellen Duggan is in good health and wishes to know from her father and Mother also

Denis Duggan wishes to know how his Dear Mother and family are and Daniel Keliher and wife Timothy Leary is all right he is in as good a health as ever he was and wishes to have his Mother make her mind easy and he would wish to know if John Reen and daughter got Married Dear Mother you well know how I proved to you at home and I expect to act so hereafter

Denis and Tade Reen Dear Mother You may be sure that we wont forget you we are in good health and with the help of God we expect do something for you after a time and John keep the children to School and tell the Scannells if they wer here that they would do first rate Dear Uncles let me know if my Sister was Delivered of a child and Likewise wher is My aunt Jude and also if ther be any person in our house and what about Dan Danihy and let us know all about the Crops

No More But remains your truly untill Death one Letter will do for us all

Daniel Guiny

(There were two postscripts.)

Mary Keeffe got two Dresses one from Mary Danihy & the other from Biddy Matt

let ye write as soon as possible and Direct your letter to Jeremiah Keliher Exchange Street Buffalo for Denis Danihy.

2

Envelope addressed

Michael Boyan Esqre., Kingwilliamstown Kanturk post office
County of Cork Ireland.
to be forwarded to Mr. Alexander MCarthy, of same place.

New York September 22nd. 1850.

My Dr. Father and Mother Brothers and Sisters

I write these few lines to you hopeing That these few lines may find
you all in as good State of health as I am in at present thank God
I Received your welcome letter To me Dated 22nd. of May which
was A Credit to me for the Stile and Elligence of its Fluent Language
but I must Say Rather Flattering My Dr. Father I must only say
that this a good place and A good Country for if one place does not
Suit A man he can go to Another and can very easy please himself
But there is one thing thats Ruining this place Especially the
Frontirs towns and Cities where the Flow of Emmigration is most
the Emmigrants has not money Enough to Take them to the Interior
of the Country which oblidges them to Remain here in York and
the like places for which Reason Causes the less demand for Labour
and also the great Reduction in wages for this Reason I would
advise no one to Come to America that would not have Some Money
after landing here that [would] Enable them to go west in case they
would get no work to do here but any man or woman without a
family are fools that would not venture and Come to this plentyful
Country where no man or woman ever Hungerd or ever will and
where you will not be Seen Naked, but I can asure you there are
Dangers upon Dangers Attending Comeing here but my Friends
nothing Venture nothing have Fortune will favour the brave have
Courage and prepare yourself for the next time that, that worthy
man Mr. Boyen is Sending out the next lot, and Come you all Together Couragiously and bid adiu to that lovely place the land of
our Birth. that place where the young and old joined Together
in one Common Union, both night and day Engaged in Innocent
Amusement, But alas. I am now Told its the Gulf of Miserary
oppression Degradetion and Ruin of evry Discription which I am
Sorry to hear of so Doleful a History to Be told of our Dr. Country
This my Dr. Father Induces me to Remit to you in this Letter 20

Dollars that is four Pounds thinking it might be Some Acquisiton to you untill you might Be Clearing away from that place all together and the Sooner the Better for Beleive me I could not Express how great would be my joy at our seeing you all here Together where you would never want or be at a loss for a good Breakfast and Dinner. So prepare as soon as possible for this will be my last Remittince untill I see you all here. Bring with you as much Tools as you can as it will cost you nothing to Bring them And as for your Clothing you need not care much But that I would like that yourself would Bring one good Shoot of Cloth that you would spare until you come here And as for Mary She need not mind much as I will have for her A Silk Dress A Bonnet and Viel according and Ellen I need not mention what I will have for her I can fit her well you are to Bring Enough

Flannels and do not form it at home as the way the wear Flannel at home and here is quiet different for which reason I would Rather that you would not form any of it untill you Come, with the Exception of whatever Quantity of Drawers you may have you can make tham at home But make them Roomly Enough But Make No Jackets

My Dr Father I am Still in the Same place but do not Intend to Stop there for the winter. I mean to Come in to New York and there Spend the winter   Thade Houlehan wrote to me Saying that if I wished to go up the Country that he would send me money but I declined so doing untill you Come and then after you Coming if you thing it may be Better for us to Remain here or go west it will be for you to judge but untill then I will Remain here   Dan Keliher Tells me that you Knew more of the House Carpentery than he did himself and he can earn from twelve to fourteen Shilling a day that is seven Shilling British and he also Tells me that Florence will do very well and that Michl can get a place Right off as you will not be In the Second day when you can Bind him to any Trade you wish And as for John he will Be Very Shortly able to Be Bound two So that I have Every Reason to Believe that we will all do will Together So as that I am sure its not for Slavery I want you to Come here no its for affording My Brothers and Sisters And I an oppertunity of Showing our Kindness and Gratitude and Comeing on your Seniour days that we would be placed in that possision that you my Dr. Father and Mother could walk about Lesuirly and Indepenly without Requireing your Labour an object which I am Sure will not fail even by Myself if I was oblidged to do it without the assistance of Brother or Sister for my Dr. Father and Mother

I am proud and happy to Be away from where the County Charges man or the poor Rates man or any other Rates man would have the Satisfaction of once Inpounding my cow or any other article of mine Oh how happy I feel and am sure to have look as The Lord had not it destined for [hole in paper probably obliterating 'me'] to get married to Some Loammun or another at home that after a few months he and I may be an Incumberance upon you or perhaps in the poor house by this, So my Dr. Father according as I had Stated to you I hope that whilst you are at home I hope that you will give my Sister Mary that privelage of Injoying herself Innocently on any occation that She pleases so far as I have said Innocently and as for my Dr. Ellen I am in Raptures of joy when I think of one day Seeing her and you all at the dock in New York and if I do not have a good Bottle of Brandy for you Awaiting your arrival its a Causion.

Well I have only to tell My Dr. Mother to Bring all her bed Close and also to bring the Kittle and an oven and have handles to them and do not forget the Smoothing Irons and Beware when you are on board to Bring some good floor and Ingage with the Captain Cook and he will do it Better for you for very little and also Bring some whiskey and give them the Cook and Some Sailors that you may think would do you any good to give them a Glass once in a time and it may be no harm

And Dr. Father when you are Comeing here if you Possiblely can Bring My Uncle Con I would Be glad that you would and I am sure he would be of the greatest acquisision to you on board and also Tell Mary Keeffe that if her Child died that I will pay her passage very Shortly and when you are Comeing do not be frightened Take Courage and be Determined and bold in your Undertaking as the first two or three days will be the worst to you and mind whatever happens on board Keep your own temper do not speak angry to any or hasty the Mildest Man has the best chance on board So you make your way with evey one and further you are to speak to Mr. Boyan and he I am sure will get one Request for you Mr. Boyan wil [l d]o it for me, when you are to Come ask Mr. Boyan [to g] ive you a few lines to the Agent or Berth Master of the Ship that will Secure to you the Second Cabin which I am sure Mr. Boyan will do and as soon as you Receive this letter write to me and let me know about every thing when you are to come and what time and state Particulars of evry thing to me and Direct as before. And if you are to come Shortly when you come to Liberpool wright to me also and let me know when you are to sail and the name of the Ship you sail in as I will be uneasy untill I get an answer

No more at present But that you will give Mr. and Mrs Boyan my best love and respect And let me know how they and family are as they would or will not Be ever Better than I would wish them to be also Mrs. Milton and Charles Mr. and Mrs. Roche and family Mr. and Mrs. day and family Mr. Walsh and as for his family I sure are all well Mr. and Mrs. Sullivan and family Mrs. O Brien Con Sheehan wife and family all the Hearlihys and familys Tim Leahy and family own Sullivan of Cariganes and family Darby Guinee and family John Calleghan and family Timothy Calleghan and family Timothy Sheehan and Mother   So no more at present form your Ever Dear and Loveing Child

Margaret MCarthy.

3

[The following letter has no address, date or formal salutation.]

Daniel Duginn of Buffalo
I Should like to Know how is Johanna Dugin and familey Honnorah Murphy and familey if Denis Towmey Comes to America I will Garintee to him to have him and us be one in table Bed and work Patrick Cronin the Same Coreneles Coffee the same that is if they make up there minds to Come and if Timothy Murphy Sends his Dater I would recommend him to Sind her I want you to Mention to me how is Dinis Murpey and familey Offer hickey and familey
    No More at Present Wee remain your True and Affectinate friends untill Deth and after if Posible

Direct youre Letter to Mr. Denis O'Danihey of Buffalo City

Ery ·[?] County State of New York

America

Write to us as quick as Posible in haiste

Buffalo City.

4

Michael Byrne from Boughill to Golding Bird Collector of Excise,
Galway.

Sept. 13th 1848.

Hon. Sir,

Sir With submission I take the liberty of writing those few lines
to you hoping to find your Honour in Good Health which leaves me
and all the Emigrants at present I am to inform you of our safe
arrival at Quebeck and we were recived most kindly at the Goverment
office. Every promises that ever your Honour made to us was
performed & Sir I have to let your Honour know that we had a safe
and speedy passage which is A Consolation to you and which I am
Bound to pray for you during my Days. I have to let you know in
Conformity that we got A free passage to Monthreal I took the
steamer from Monthreal to the lands of liberty And which I am to
Inform your Honour that I am Employed in the rail road line earning
5s. a day of your Irish money And instead of being chained with
poverty in Boughill I am crowned with glory and so I bless the day
that you had come to Boughill And when I cannot return you no
other thanks I write theese few lines of pleasure to you in Adoption
to you and Family And I am better pleased to come to this country
than if you bestowed me five Acres of land in Boughill.

I have to let your Honour know that all the Emigrants of Boughill
has send you their best respect and blessing And we are in hopes
that we will never die intil we see you once more And as this is
A letter of pleasure to you I hope you will let the tenants of Boughill
know of our safe arrival in America.

And as it is my first writing to you I am to let you know that I
am Employed in Section 35 rail road lines Middlebury post office
state of Vermounth.

No more at present but we all join in sending our loving friendship
to you untill Death

I remain your most respectfully Micke [?] Byrne And I am your
Humble and obedient Servient Michael Byrne.

This is Michael Killelea his hand writing Matheis[?] Killelea
his son

To Golding Bird Esqure
Galway